THROUGH AMY'S EYES

INSIGHT PUBLICA

Nadakkavu, Kozhikode, Kerala, 673011
www.insightpublica.com
e-mail: insightpublica@gmail.com
Title: **Through Amy's Eyes**
Author: **Abeer Ashraf**
First Insight Edition:
Cover & Layout: kjvj@insight

Printed and Published by
InsightinPublica Printers & Publishers Pvt. Ltd.
ISBN ISBN 978-93-5517-411-6

THROUGH AMY'S EYES

ABEER ASHRAF

INSIGHT PUBLICA®

Abeer Ashraf was born and raised in Jeddah, Saudi Arabia, except for the time she moved to Kerala, India to pursue her higher studies. She began writing at a young age about everything she could. Her high school textbooks are filled with poetry and thoughts of whatever comes across her mind. She began writing this debut novel of hers during the covid-19 pandemic. Writing is her escape. It distracts her mind when needed and engages it in the best possible way. When she's not writing, she can be found studying, wandering through quiet places, or just engaged in tons of other activities. But even during all those distracted times, no other activity brings in as much joy and inner peace as writing does for her.

Abeer Ashraf
Nilambur,
Kerala, India
abeerashrafhere@gmail.com

From the Author

Ever since I can remember, writing has always been my passion. To be able to express one's feelings, thoughts and imagination through words… is fascinating to me. After years of contemplation, I finally present to you my first published novel.

Growing up, every kid has their phase with a variety of genre of their liking. Personally I've always preferred fictional mystery novels. Crime thrillers being my perfect cup of tea.

They bring in that little something that's missing in one's imagination. Hopefully I was able to achieve what I was going for through this crime thriller novel. Being it my first work, it might not knock your shoes off but it will definitely be worth your while! I guess, what I am trying to say is…

Dearest Reader,

Enjoy.

CONTENTS

CHAPTER I

Amy Gwenith Smith, a smart but silent child- known as a shadow to most kids her age, for she did not care to have unwanted popularity or a lot of friendships. She had a peculiar something about her though. One would always feel her presence around coz' she would catch your eye but not enough to do anything about it. These are of course only the calculated thoughts of her classmates. How could one possibly know what she is up to right now- for nobody's heard from her or seen her in a long time.

DAY 16 since Amy

Jenna and Mark seem pretty confused on all the mismatched puzzle pieces of this very unsettling case. Not to mention how they've been hurdled upon other missing persons cases that could be linked to this one.

"Ok, hold on a minute Mark- How is this possible? How is not a single person having any idea or a clear picture of a teenage girl who has been living under their own noses her entire life?!"

With no breath to catch with all the heat that's been riled up in detective Jenna's mind, she takes it out on her newbie partner Mark and returns to the interviews of Amy's supposed family and friends.

"Yes ma'am, you were saying something that happened on May 7th, what was it now?"

Mark led the interview this time with Amy's homeroom teacher Mrs. Susanne.

"Oh why yes, Amy... you see... she's the silent kind, you know, the one that's of least trouble and bother..... Stood out the least too. But on May 7th, was it...yes... I remember because I was supposed to be out of town that day but yea... on that day, she was- different. Or shall I say disturbed? At first, I thought it'd be natural for anyone to finally have a breakdown... especially since Stella's disappearance in Amy's case. I would've lost it long before had it been my best friend missing too. But Amy- she... she kept her calm since the news first came out and I just felt like something's there? - More to it I mean... like a cause, you know. Maybe a trigger? For she did lose her cool that day pretty bad..."

"By lost her cool- what exactly do you mean?"

"She threw a fit in the classroom. Apparently there was nothing out of the blue and everyone... they were getting ready for the next class and all of a sudden...Amy started screaming, banging her head on the table... and... here's the weird part- laughing. I honestly didn't know what to do so I took her directly into the counselor's room right away. I feel sorry now... what she did did scare the kids around her and I was too focused on them that I couldn't pay enough attention to Amy herself. If I could've done something that day... anything at all... that day was the last time I saw her too. She didn't return to class after that. I keep thinking to myself if I could've done something- if I could've made a better choice- would things be different right now....."

Slightly sobbing Mrs. Susanne caught Jenna's annoyed eye-

"And what choice would that be ma'am?"

Jenna lost her patience on what was clearly a pre-rehearsed

show going on in front of her. Mrs. Susanne stuttered for words as she tried to reply to Jenna.

"What? No, I meant... for the sake of Amy... I could have- I should have-"

"Yes ma'am, I think we've got everything we need for now. We'll contact you again- do stay in touch. Not to mention... no out of town trips and of course, calling us when there is something out of the ordinary. Thank you for coming in."

Mark's reassuring tone somehow soothed Susanne's mind after Jenna's sudden interrogative switch of atmosphere.

Back at the station, however everything was a Mayhem- but coming back to the chaos and reporting back to their superiors is an inevitable thing for detectives like Jenna and Mark. It seems to be a never ending cat and the mouse chase with the possible suspects' list lengthening after each interview.

"Oh, how easy the movies and dramas portray investigative thrillers. Where are all the magically solved puzzles and hints and easily caught culprits whenever you need them?"

Jenna's inner thoughts line up one after the other trying to find a hint or a missing bit or a piece of information that could help them in this case but in reality it was like trying to find a needle in a haystack.

"By the way Mark, any news on Louis? Where did our prime suspect vanish into, anyways? With all these priors... how'd he manage to go off the grid with little to no trace of him left behind? Weird how he managed to disappear right before his daughter disappeared too. They possibly cannot be in cahoots or anything right? Or shall we say, perfectly coincidentally planned... Ahhh!! Any news about him yet?"

"Am afraid not... But hey Jen- it's his step daughter. There's motive and clear history of violence between Louis and both Linda and Amy and not to mention his criminal background. Why don't we just pick this path and hold this case till Louis turns up again?"

"So he can go around making more missing girls cases for detectives like us? That is.... if he is the person we are after... I mean, we could be climbing up the wrong tree after all! Let's take a break... collect up our stuff and start from the beginning again... now... had anything to eat yet?"

"Ummmm... we've both been together since the afternoon and its half past 11 right now, I guess we forgot about our hunger amidst all this...."

(Grrrr- apparently Mark's stomach remembers)

Jenna laughs at embarrassed Mark-

"Let's go get something to eat and start fresh."

"Wait, aren't you going home after? It's already past our overtime"

"Ah... yea... okay. Let's meet in the morning to discuss the rest of it, I guess. Anyways... who all were coming in tomorrow again? - for the interview"

"Yea, we have Linda coming in again, also some of Amy's classmates- Milinca's coming tomorrow too...."

The night deepens as they try going over the case's details even after going off the clock.

DAY 17 since Amy

"Hey Jen... Linda's here...."

The first thing in the morning to be Mark's unexpected announcement of the victim's mother awaiting answers for her missing daughter was not how Jenna wanted to start her day.

Nevertheless here goes nothing…literally. Considering the point of trying to give a sense of hope to the scared and clueless mother. Just as Jenna's eyes met Linda's puffed dried up eyes that's obviously been through a lot for the past 17 days, Jenna regretted going home and resting, when the woman in front of her have been restless for days. She regretted having nothing to console Linda with- not a single piece of information that could ease her mind about her daughter.

"Linda, hey, let's talk over here"

Jenna took Linda by her hand to the empty desk in the corner of the room knowing some quiet and helping hands will do her good.

"I'm sorry for not calling you back- it's just been a lot of work you see. Am sorry for not having much to update you about Amy's whereabouts either. We really are trying our best. We just need some more-"

Cutting her off mid-sentence, Linda took over.

"Meet my eyes when you speak to me please."

She caught Jen trying to avoid eye contact, for Jen was clearly trying to bluff her way out of this very interaction and skip to the part of questions. Linda spoke again, breaking the thick silence after her remark-

"I know you all are all I've got. I have put my trust in you. I'll survive knowing you will find her. Till that day, I'll keep moving on. Do not worry about me. I just need you to find her. Please."

Sobbing now with tears flowing down her face, she paused for a minute and grabbed Jenna's hands and with sad hopeful eyes she asked,

"What about Stella? Any news about her? Am sure she will know where Amy is. Please- I know they had some kind of a fight but if you ask her over and over again, she'll give in. Even if it means not revealing about her present stay and stuff to us or her parents. Just please persuade her to tell you about Amy because she'd know. She always knew."

That last sentence strike Jen-

"What do you mean by always know Linda? You mean, this is not the first time Amy's gone missing?"

Wiping off her tears to clarify her statement, Linda replied with a restless tone-

"No, no, it's not like that. Amy's never been missing. Before. She just didn't come home for a few days- that's because-"

Jen exclaimed with a deep sigh-

"Ahhh! Linda! I told you not to keep anything from us! How often did Amy show this behavior? Why did you think of hiding this from us? How did you think this will help-"

"WHAT DO YOU MEAN BY THIS BEHAVIOUR? There is no behavior. She was never gone before. That time was 3 days and it was all because of Louis. I knew she left. I knew she'd be ok. I knew she was going to come back to me! I know she is going to come back to me this time too! But you have to listen to me. 17 DAYS. 17 DAYS IS WHAT. I haven't seen my girl... my Amy... for 17 days. If her past comes up for you to take it up as an excuse to not find her and just move on by ignoring my girl's call for help. I swear to all of you- NONE OF YOU WILL GET AWAY WITH THIS. Don't you even think for a second that just because I have nobody come in for me... I'd leave in peace with all of you screwing this case over!"

Mark to the rescue of the screaming out of patience Linda calmed her down by bringing her back to the desk once again and assured her that they will find her daughter no matter what.

Jenna was right beside him but couldn't muster up the courage to say anything- for it could all be misinterpreted once again. Linda couldn't stop crying after this and had no words to spare... Jenna got up to give her some space and to get some fresh air for herself.

Just as she was about to get out, an unfamiliar voice called out for her-

"Detective Jones? Jenna Jones?"

Turning around with a headache that's already been spiked up, Jenna was surprised to see an unfamiliar face calling out for her. All of a sudden she recognized the face. Milinca. Milinca in middle of all of this was unexpected.

Jenna remembered her clearly... for when they visited

Amy's school a while ago, she noticed Milinca following both her and Mark around all along as if she had something to say but when Jenna tried to approach her, she walked away. That was one of the reasons why Milinca was called in separately on request.

Gathering up her mind once again, Jenna managed to click right into action.

"Yes, Milinca was it? Ummm- let's talk over here"

Mark noticed how Jenna and Milinca were headed to the interrogation room but didn't want to leave Linda's side just yet. So he let them be.

Judging by how nervous and troubled Milinca looked and how she voluntarily came up for this interview and how she managed to call out for Jen amidst all the chaos around, one thing was made clear- she needed to come here. Only question is… why? What is she looking for? Or is she here with a critical piece of information?

Focused on Milinca's trembling eyes, Jenna started the session.

"Hello Milinca, this is just a basic interview we are holding for all of Amy's friends and family, so you don't need to be worried or anything. All you need to do is answer a few questions"

"-Ok... by the way, she's not my friend."

"Excuse me?"

"Amy- she's not my friend. We are not close enough to be friends."

Perplexed by how Milinca was randomly stating reasons for her to not be here but still being present in this scenario made Jen a little confused.

"-Ok? What was your relationship with Amy then? How'd you know her?"

"I actually don't. Not Amy at least."

After a moment or two, Milinca sat up straight, placed her hands on the desk, met Jenna's eyes and started to say what she was really here for.

"You see detective, before Amy... we've noticed a few girls missing too. Only difference is Amy was out of the blue. Before her, everyone that disappeared were cut off completely and labelled as runaways. For no damn reason too. How easy it was for all the adults to move on with their lives after just ignoring something that is obviously not right! I mean, how are we supposed to be ok with all of this? How are we supposed to ignore all this when it is happening right before us-"

Cutting off the so very hot speech Milinca was going on about, Jenna interrupted with even more confusing questions than ever.

"Hey, hey Milinca... what are you talking about? Before Amy, there were more girls missing? Who? You were close with any of them?"

With a sudden change of tone in Milinca's hot tempered state, she frowned... stared down at her own feet... and whispered under her breath-

"Stella."

Wow, well that broke the cold giant ice in the room for Jen. That's the second time someone's mentioned her name in the past hour. Funny thing is... of course, nobody's seen Stella either.

With a deep sigh, Jenna asked Milinca

"And how do you know Stella? What is it you're really trying to say here now? We know nobody's heard from Stella in a while too but we've got witnesses who've seen her boarding buses and her own parents testify that she frequently goes off the grid as she likes. What seems suspicious to you about Stella anyway?"

"No, no, you see detective, that's it. Everybody thinks she

just dropped off school and everything because she does it often... But no! You see, she was an open book. She spoke to literally anyone and was friendly to almost everyone. And she's mentioned how... no matter how fun and exciting going off the grid is, she always lets someone know about her plans. Coz' she had experienced something dark it seems. Usually it's Amy who knows... coz' you see, she was always by her side... weirdly... like they were some sort of stuck-in-partners or something. But there were times when they'd be on bad terms... and Stella would spill it to me."

"Spill? You mean, she tells you about her runaway plans?"

"No, not runaway plans. It's not like that. She just goes somewhere to free her mind and get some air... you know."

"You could do that with all the space available around here kid, now did she tell you where she'd go this time too or no?"

"That's the thing detective. She didn't. And I thought Amy would know. As far as we knew, there was nothing wrong with them. No fights, arguments or anything. So I asked Amy about it myself. She pretended to not show it but she was genuinely surprised to hear that I didn't know where she was either. That's when I knew. That's when I saw it. Amy squandered a bit in front of me to avoid talking to me and rushed home that day. I thought it was all just a big hassle coz it was obvious Amy and Stella had some kind of a fight and Amy just didn't want to talk about it or something. But two days later, Amy... she... she came to class all drenched. It was as if someone beat her up real bad. We assumed it was just her stepdad going overboard on her again... but never the less I approached her... and just as I touched her shoulders- she lost it. She started screaming and acting all –weird? I got scared myself so I moved away. But I heard her say something. She laid her head down on the table and wept pretty hard. In midst of her weeping and weird laughing... I heard her whisper... something like... I'm sorry Stella or... You should be sorry Stella... I couldn't hear it clearly coz she was taken away to

the counselor's room after that."

"Let me get this straight. You heard her say I'm sorry or you should be sorry Stella? I'm supposed to buy this-why?"

"I know you have no good reason to believe what I'm saying right now, but trust me on one thing please. Whatever happened to Amy or wherever she is... it is related to Stella. It's just something you need to trust me on. Please. Find Stella... Oh... And Amy."

Jenna was half convinced on how Milinca was still hiding something from her. But she already kind of scared off Milinca before, at the school and had no way of finding out more about this if she were to go away again. So she decided to flip a coin on fate and buy her story.

Blinded by trust or not, Jenna didn't see how following up on this lead could backfire in any way.

"Yes, Milinca, am sorry for losing my cool. I'll make sure to look into Stella and do everything I can to bring both of them back. I hope you have let me know about everything you know that could help us in any way. I hope you're not keeping anything... not even a small piece of information from us."

Just as Jenna remarked about not hiding anything from her, Milinca's eyes met Jenna's and with a sudden tremble of fear, she avoided Jenna's eyes and looked away. Stating the obvious, Jenna asked one last time,

"Is there anything more you'd like to let me know? If it can help your friends... am sorry... friend and classmate in anyway, I suggest you open up right now!"

Trembling eyes, uneasy breath, eyes shifting from one side of the room to the other, Milinca's entire body was speaking unintentionally.

In an attempt of trying to break her, Jenna stood up and acted as if she was about to leave losing patience. Just as she was about to exit the room....

"Wait... there's more. I'm... I'm not sure if this would

help...but ... and I don't know more about it as well. I just know that it happened... but I don't know who... or how... or even whose fault it was... I just-"

Cutting her off to make her stop beating around the bush, Jenna asked her to get to the point right away.

Milinca just stared at the ground, her nails tightly marking the inner palms of her wrists.

Seeing how she still hesitated and was not giving in- Jenna walked towards the door once again and just as she grabbed the handle of the door-

-*"she was raped."*

CHAPTER II

DAY 22 since Amy

The world seems to be a wrecked piece of land covered in mine bombs for Jenna and somehow she managed to be the only one stepping on every single one of them.

Every single time they get close to finding something or following up a lead- they face a hurdle only to end up right back at square one.

It was about to be a week since Jen heard the possibility of one of the missing girls to be abused. Even after a week worth of search parties… Patrol groups… and countless headhunting… these kids- they remain missing.

"Hey Jen, remember the department store we asked around about Louis a few days ago- looks like we finally caught a break."

In an instance of critical timing, Mark came with an inch of good news for Jen. Their initial hunt for the most suspicious person among their suspects' list finally has a lead.

"The department store owner called in a few times asking for you it seems. Looks like he found something weird through the security camera footages."

All of a sudden, this day seems to be surreal to Jen. Everything she'd wanted to hear for the past 22 days were coming from Mark. It's almost like a Jenga tower being built up with so much hope only to have it fall over in a moment's time. Coming back to her consciousness, she asked Mark:

"Wait what? We went through all the footage ourselves. We couldn't find anything about Louis after May 8th, did we? How come there's new footage all of a sudden?"

A relieved and surprised Jen sounded rude but was only confused and somewhat happy to get something to hold onto finally.

"Yea Jen, apparently it's not about Louis. But something we need to see. So I guess we need to get going-"

Before he could finish his sentence, Jenna already grabbed her keys and started heading out.

On the way out, as expected- more hurdles for Jen to overcome. Linda's back again. Her helplessness and washed out face always looked pitiful but she managed to kick off any soft feelings from the officers at the station by showing up at the station and causing a scene. every. single. day.

Even though she knew the gravity of the situation- she just couldn't help herself. At first, she used to come in and have a riot all by herself. But now that she has realized how that only prolonged this deep torment to herself and wasted all of Jenna's and Mark's time and effort... She changed her approach.

These days Linda is just present at the station with a calm maintained posture on the outside and a complete mess on the inside.

She is just around for answers. Little does she know her desperate measures is affecting Jenna and Mark way more than it should!

Of course, it is only natural for the victim's mother to be as troubled as Linda is- but it should be understood on how the depth of the matter affects the detectives in charge too.

Avoiding any sort of communication or contact with Linda

to prevent any chance of false hopes or misinterpretation, Jen and Mark head straight out, paying no attention to the desperately pacing Linda who was about to approach them to ask where they were off to.

At the department store, to their surprise, the owner had already set up the copy of the footage for them to go over. And guess what? There's no Louis in sight. But here's the part that caught the owner's eye, also Jenna's-

On May 8th Louis enters the store alone, unaccompanied by no one. 17 minutes later, exits after purchasing a pack of cigarettes but with a friendly stranger? Or was it a coincidental meeting of two acquaintances?

"And who is this pretty mystery man that slipped our eyes?"

Mark only said out loud what Jenna was thinking.

The mystery man that followed Louis out seems to be someone who's new to this whole scenario.

Starting fresh back at the station on a new lead but with less despair on their side, Jenna and Mark were hopeful once again.

Finding the mystery man's identity was a piece of cake alright! Apparently an infamous photographer of some sort is not so hard to track down- or so it happens to be.

To get in touch with him however, Jenna and Mark were in a bit of a twirl. There's no available active number, home address, studio address or anything of the sort registered under his name except for a roughly put up website.

Going in for the long shot- they sent in a message at the viewer's private comment section hoping to hear back soon. Obviously if that doesn't work, they'll have to go on another sweet but bitter journey of finding this so called Christopher Lynn- if that even is his real name.

On a quest to find more leverage on this Christopher Lynn person, binge watching saga began for Jen and Mark. Only the series they'll be binging is a month's worth of CCTV footage of a department store.

"Yea Jen, while we were at that store, we should've got popcorn for this"

"We should've overseen our pretty movie date- yea."

Suddenly changing the tone back to the default detective Jenna version-

"By the way, when did Linda leave? Anything she started up here or something?"

"Yea, she left right after we headed out to the store. Apparently she didn't cause much of a scene- so all good? For now?"

Why did Mark's reply only seem to trouble Jen more? Guilt perhaps? But, Jen has nothing to be guilty for.

Except, every time Jenna sees poor Linda, day by day, unable to console her or provide her with some sort of comforting news or anything about her missing child- one cannot help but feel guilty.

"A mother's cry for help- how long can I keep ignoring her cry without having to deal with this feeling of guilt. How long must she suffer... for any mother shouldn't be going through this..."

-Jenna's dark thoughts started to consume her yet once again- but she couldn't let that happen. If she did, it'll only add on more darkness to her life. So she clicked right out of it and got straight to business.

The dawn passed right before their eyes as they scourged through hours long of videos and found out every trace of Christopher that they could.

Surprises on surprises as they've caught a big one this time.

Mark put up his sheet on the case board first. Jenna put hers up right next to it. Guess what- every day Louis went into that store before May 8th- Christopher was there too. And after Louis' disappearance, Christopher has managed to keep up his appearance every Tuesday of every week. Not the best part yet. With a new profound grin on Jen's face, she says-

"Christopher Lynn, our very mysterious stranger, comes into the store, every Tuesday, 6:30 on the dot and exits before its 7 with just the exact same five things purchased- cigarettes, 6 bottles of water, 2 packs of cotton gauze, masking tape and a pair of gloves. How so very fitting for unsuspicious very normal human behavior."

Mark played along

"Seems like we've got another main photograph to get signed now, besides Louis. Except both of them are of course out of our reach."

"Well, at least not for long. Tomorrow's Tuesday."

Jenna's statement caught Mark off guard. He looked at the time and realized,

"You mean, today?"

DAY 23 since Amy

Digging into Christopher Lynn's data of all kinds- Jenna and Mark got pretty neat with his background. Now the only question that remains, how do they link these victims to the suspect? Trying to get back at their speed taking a break after pulling an all-nighter, Jen and Mark began thinking ahead,

"I mean, all this started as a missing persons case. There was no evidence to believe otherwise- no kidnapping scenes, ransom calls or anything of the sort. So if we do bring Christopher in, what for? What can we say for actually bringing him in? I mean... suspicious behavior at a store cannot actually keep our suspect in here forever now. And when he knows we've got nothing but hunches, he's got no reason to stay either. Also, what are we going to report to the chief if it goes that way, Jen?

The person that was supposedly feeding Jenna with ear

candy the day before seems to be more of a headache today.

"So what exactly are you suggesting Mark? Let this man be? And let this case go on as just as a missing person's case- that's obviously headed to be labelled as a cold case... forever? It's been more than 20 days. Missing person cases are usually dealt with by this time, but with what we have been through these past few weeks- we know there is more to this. We can't just abandon this case without following up on every single lead there is. Even if it means treating this case as any other case- kidnapping, murder, or anything of that importance... For we are not giving up on these kids. Not when it literally looks like everyone else did."

Frustrated with all the heat fueled up in Jen, she took a breath and added,

"We cannot give up now... not when we are finally this close... not without an answer for her..."

Glancing at Linda who's been sitting at the station for hours, Jenna and Mark decide to go all in and starts plotting their game plan to bring in Christopher.

As far as their research, Christopher lives out of this world- both socially and by law. There's not a single record of any law breaking or a social media trace of the guy. However, the guy was quite friendly. The people he surrounded himself with from time to time are quite active and there's plenty of photo evidence for that. Especially with the ladies- quite a famous fellow.

Of course, the common ground on all of these people's interaction with Christopher... was not having anything common about it at all. All of them. Literally every single one of them had no ties or connection with him before or after their one and only interaction. Or so Jenna and Mark had to believe with what they could gather from the people that he met. And for these ladies he was just a friendly stranger who was hot enough for a single meet and then back to strangers again, coz' apparently he never left any crumbs behind… on how to stay in touch. So that leaves that- but quite an image for this alienated fellow, isn't it?

Determined to have this Christopher person come in as soon as possible, Jenna and Mark prepare themselves for meeting him at the store- not too long from now.

Time clicking away, anxiety levels on the check, all ready to go in, Jenna and Mark patiently wait at the parking lot in front of the store.

Minutes later, entry of the estranged mystery man and less than 30 meters away, awaits Jenna and Mark who's looking for Christopher to enter the store for them to go in and approach him… and eventually convince him to come in to the station for collecting his statement.

Just then, right in front of the store's entry- Christopher stops. It looked as if he was hesitant to go into the store.

A perplexed Jenna did not know what he was doing and looked at Mark to see if he knew what was going on. Staring at each other and then back at Christopher, they noticed how he impatiently kept looking at his mobile phone. Now that. That caught their attention.

No trace of a mobile phone found for this person and here he stands in front of their eyes- holding one- or more precisely, waiting for some sort of a response or call or something.

Growing more anxious of the situation, Mark decides to go out and approach him anyway. Stopping Mark, Jenna says,

"Let's see what he does, we have him now anyways. He's right in front of us. Let us just keep our pace and see what he does or where he'll lead us to. So let's just stay put."

Just as she finished speaking, Mark starts the car, coz' of course, Christopher was on the move.

He turns back, gets into a taxi and started moving. Mark and Jenna followed right behind. Following him, Jenna felt like this was too familiar- the way they were headed to. Just as she knew for sure, they took the turn and saw Christopher getting off the car.

To everybody's surprise, the very place they all stand within right now is nowhere other than the station itself. The station that Jen and Mark left a few hours ago in order to find and apprehend Christopher.

"Now what does this mean, Jen?"

A very perplexed Mark did not know how to react to this situation.

Jen on the other hand had something else on her mind. She was ready to have it. If this is the game she has to play to finally get somewhere with her case- she'll play it. But she'll make sure to win it too.

With a new mindset set to restart this scenario that has now turned tables- they enter the station right behind Christopher.

Into the battlefield all of them enter, each strategized and all ready to take each other out.

Christopher was at the front desk and asking around about something when Jenna and Mark entered and the officer at the desk called out for them. Just as they predicted, he was in asking for them.

Christopher locked eyes with Mark and Jen.

"Yes, detective Jones? I was asked to meet with detective Jones? I did write back to know the reason but didn't hear anything, so I'm here to find out- I guess."

He sounded firm- as if he'd come prepared. And of course, Jen guessed that much as well. Seemingly surprised on how it slipped their minds to check the message dashboard of his website, they knew he had the upper hold of the present situation. And knowing that much, Jen put on her game face as well.

"Hello Christopher, sorry we were just caught up in work. We just wanted you to come in for a routine interview, answer

a couple of questions, that's all. If that's ok by you- I mean."

"Interview? Questions? Am I a suspect in a case or something?"

He chuckled lightly making his remark.

"Not exactly Mr. Lynn. You just need to come with us and have a nice little chat- that's it for now."

Mark replied mocking his laugh as well.

23 days later, finally catching a break, Jenna and Mark had a potential suspect in the interrogation room.

The mind games began. Mark laid out the photographs of Amy, Stella and Louis on the table and asked him if he knew any one of them.

To their surprise, he picked out one of them without any hesitation. The steadiness in his posture and tone seemed to be too perfectly aligned- raising even more suspicion.

"Why is Stella's picture over here?"

'Why does every single person we've ever spoken to, know or verify their relationship or connection with Stella' – Telepathically conveying the same message, Jenna and Mark looked at each other with the exact same expression.

Judging by how Jenna and Mark reacted to his question, Christopher asked,

"I guess it's not Stella you're after, after all... Huh..."

That caught Jenna's attention. It was as if he was indirectly hinting on something he already knew that they know.

"Mr. Lynn, we'd appreciate it if you only answered our questions and not draw any conclusions of your own. Now, how do you know Stella?"

"Ok detective, my bad. I just don't know why a nice little girl like Stella is being brought up in some questioning with the cops- especially with me- that's why I assumed the other pictures were whom you guys were actually after. By the way, Stella's a friend. We met through some party I guess. Yea,

that's all"

"That's all? Christopher- right. How exactly did you meet a nice little girl in some party and become friends? And you don't know the people in these pictures? They don't even look slightly familiar to you?"

Mark took over for Jen. He needed answers and was ready to get them in a haste.

Christopher started to speak hesitantly

"Ummm... Stella was someone I met through a party yea, I don't remember when or which one but we've been to a few more parties together so we became friends like that. Am sorry, am I in some kind of trouble here? I thought I was just here to answer a few of your questions. Why does this feel more like an interrogation?"

"Hey now, we are only asking basic questions here of course, and you are only answering them- no need to jump into any conclusions all right."

After taking a moment to realize Mark pushed Christopher a bit too hard, Jenna asked again,

"So you are saying you don't know any of these people in the photograph?"

"Yea, I mean... I don't recall their faces."

As expected, he lied but without showing it. Jen and Mark were prepared of course. Without wasting much time beating around the bush, they took out another photo- the one from the camera footage at the store, showing both Louis and Christopher all friendly and walking out of the store together.

Placing it on the table, Jenna asked,

"How would you explain this then?"

Christopher's eyes shifted from the photo on the table to Jenna's eyes, back to the photo and then at Mark.

Obviously caught off guard, he tried to play it cool by saying

"Oh, was that the same guy in the other photo? I guess I did meet him then. But how am I supposed to know a person I met at some store? It's not like I know everybody I've ever met in my life."

Christopher shrugged his shoulders and fixed his posture once again.

What a sight to witness- thought Jenna with a smirk. Seeing Christopher trying to wiggle his way out through excuses… and up next, she turned on a video on her laptop and showed it to Christopher.

"And do you talk to every 'stranger from the store' like you've been friends with them from before… perhaps like this?"

Christopher knew what was coming now. He could see it in Jenna's eyes how he wouldn't be spared.

He did come in with a plan after all- and when his plan A seemed to not be working, he decides to switch over to plan B. With a new look on his face and a smile out of nowhere-

"Alright detectives, you got me. Guess I should've known you've done your homework. Yes, that's Louis. I can't exactly say I know him, but I guess I can say I don't not know him- so yea. Is that all?"

Jenna and Mark were perplexed as of what just happened. They'd expected Christopher to have a plan but admitting and lowering his shield about Louis all of a sudden with a slight trigger, now that got them flustered. They didn't know what he was plotting. But their doubts couldn't stop this now… as he already started speaking about Louis, Jenna and Mark was ready to explore more about it.

As heat bottled up in the room with a lot of questions arising and not a lot of easy answers given away.

Jenna, Mark and Christopher sit across each other, staring at one another with a lot of unsaid words being said like they knew where they're headed to with the conversation they were about to have.

"Ok, we can either go the long way, with you only adding onto your jail time or start talking already to help yourself out here."

Mark started to lose patience and let Christopher in on some good advice.

Christopher was less relaxed as compared to before, but still maintained his posture of put-up calmness and thought he'd had the upper hold this time and thought of having things his way.

He decided to play around after all. Firstly by playing dumb on why Louis was wanted and then acting all tough but eventually just adding on more dirt about Louis in it all and giving in more leverage on Louis alone, to Jenna and Mark.

In all the acts he was putting on, Jenna kept calm and when she noticed Mark was about to lose it a few times, she lightly held his hands as a sign to let it off and stay put. She knew he'd just go on and there was no need for them to trick him into their trap. All they had to do was patiently wait and listen up to him having a slip of tongue. He hasn't mentioned Amy's name or anything about her connecting him to the case after all.

Louis' name was all over his speech. The more he went on, the more he purposefully let them in about everything Louis could be incriminated for.

Of course, the pattern was forming. Christopher's plan was just plainly visible to Jenna now.

He was only having one goal from the start. His only aim for coming in at all. He brought all this on… made all these curves only to reach this exact place- giving Louis away.

It was as if he just wanted Louis to be taken in already, as if he was under some curse by Louis that could only be broken with him gone.

Jenna had it all figured out now.

Christopher was the errand boy. He was only fetching for Louis. He wanted to break away from his master and the only way he'd achieve that was if Louis gets imprisoned- and that's where Jenna and Mark come in.

The only question that remained for Jen however was,

"How did Christopher get entangled in all of this in the first place? Christopher mentioned about how Louis sold drugs and stuff but even if Christopher was involved in that, there's not enough reason for him to betray Louis now... Now, what does Louis have over Christopher that he has to take these big risky measures to get Louis locked up and make sure whatever Louis has on him doesn't come out?"

Jenna knew now that that's where she should begin. That should be the topic of his confession next. For we did get what he was trying to do with all of the Louis did that and Louis did this talk.

While the so very oblivious Christopher took a break from his own talk show feeling as if everything was going exactly according to his plan, Jenna interrupts his bittersweet thoughts,

"So tell me Christopher, how exactly did you meet Louis?"

Christopher's entire aura switched. His satisfied smile started to fade away, having faced with an unexpected dilemma.

According to him, the detectives were supposed to be more than pleased by all the information he had fed them... there was no reason to start digging into him again. But now that things started to turn the way he didn't expect it do, he slowly started to get lost.

He looked at Jenna, then with an uncomfortable laugh said,

"Yea, that's a funny story I guess. We met through the store I think... something he'd wanted to buy and I ran into him or something-"

"Doesn't seem to be the exact funny one you intended... why don't you try again?"

Jenna cut him off with a profound wicked smile coz' she knew she had him. Stumbling for words, Christopher was way more careful with his words now,

"Ha...Now that I think about it, I guess we met through some people in our common circle or something... friends of-"

Jenna didn't wait for him to finish to cut him off again.

"Common circle, friends... nope, try again and try better!"

Starting to get flustered, a very annoyed Christopher started to get a hang of the situation that was taking place in front of him.

He was hiding something and he knew they knew it too.

He sat up, loosened his legs, and freely formed his position on the chair he's been sitting on for a long time. He put his hands in his pockets and all of a sudden, got up.

Standing up straight, staring at Jenna, Christopher was ready to walk out on them.

Mark got up too, thinking he was going to make a run for it.

Just as all the uncertainties filled up the room, Jenna spoke to break it up one by one,

"Mr. Christopher Lynn, while you try to figure out what you're next move will be or what your next story would be about, let me remind you- we found you. We will find whatever it is you are hiding too. We will get to it either way, so why don't you chill, sit back down and let us know about everything yourself... that way, even if it's not as much as useful towards you, I can say it'd do you less harm- probably. Now, why don't you begin with how you met Louis Smith?"

The tables had turned. Jenna was the calm one with a psychopathic tone and Christopher was out of cards to play. Knowing his defeat, realizing how there were no more moves left for him, he slowly sat back down. He finally decided to give in, surrender and move on with what could be done as damage control.

A completely different side of Christopher was on display in front of Jenna and Mark as of right now. Knowing he'll eventually start speaking in a matter of time, they patiently waited.

Finally, Christopher started talking. Shoulders shrugged, eyes fixated on his own feet, helplessly rested hands on his knees, he said,

"It was all because of Stella... I... we... met in a party and we gradually got closer. That's how she introduced Amy to me as well. It was nothing serious for me, but I guess she felt different. I guess I didn't want to break off from her as well, so I put up with all of her clinginess and stuff. She used to hang around me all the time and slowly by time, Amy was also frequently around. That's when I started noticing... that's how I got involved... Amy used to turn up looking like a beaten up sand bag most days and when I finally realized it was her own stepdad causing it, I thought of getting in and confronting him. Stella was the one who encouraged me as well. Amy on the other hand, didn't know... I showed up at her house and when Amy saw me, she dragged out and saw Stella out and went all nuts at us... That's when Louis came out, he started going on about how Amy's got people to take care of her or something and eventually... we did get into a fight..."

"Louis and you? When was this by the way?"

"Yea, about two months ago maybe? He did get me pretty good and Amy never showed up near me after that. Stella was all tense around me after that day too... I was already planning on ending things with her of course, so this made things easy. We were done after that."

"You mean, you and Stella broke up?"

"Yes. I thought I'd never get back in touch with any of them afterwards, coz' I usually don't- but I did. Stella reached out to me a while ago... sounded all scared and stuff... but didn't tell me what the reason was over the phone... so I went over

to meet her..."

"She did call you then? But, you have no mobile number or service registered to you or anything of the sort. How'd that happen again?"

"Yea, it's not mine... I don't own any number or a cellphone for that matter. I just got this from a friend a while ago, not for any specific reason but yea... eventually...this stuck around with me."

"Wait a minute, is this the number you own perhaps?"

Mark showed a number from his notepad and asked about it.

"Yea, why do you have it written down?"

Mark and Jen looked at each other after Christopher's reply and started to get a gist of everything happening. Mark replied to him however,

"You were the last person to speak to Stella."

A confused Christopher was shocked to hear that.

"Wh- what? I mean... yea, I know she's not been home for the past couple of days but no calls? That's not possible- I mean... that's not what he said to me... Louis I mean..."

"Louis? He spoke to Stella?"

Jenna was getting more confused on how things were coming up all mixed.

"Yea... Louis... that day Stella wanted to meet. I went over to the parking lot of that store, that's where we usually meet... but she wasn't there. I looked around and she wasn't there. Just as I was about to leave, Louis turned up. He took me to the corner and beat me up. I'd thought he was just going on about the grudge from before. But this time, after beating me up, he made me stand back up and laughed. Then he said if I don't work with him and do as he says, Stella's gona come back into my life but this time she's gona come back for revenge and that he'd be right there with her."

"So you're saying Louis was there on behalf of Stella? Coz' she told him to get you or something?"

"I don't know! I mean, I used to think of it that way. I thought if I played by what she says or what he says- I'll get out eventually... but yea, this just kept going on and on... twice a week, maybe thrice, he'd call me up and make me buy stuff for him. Random weird stuff. But the same thing over and over again. I thought this was all just a way for Stella to toy with me. But then, one day I asked him. I asked Louis why he was taking orders from Stella. That's when he lost it. He beat me up again and went on about how he takes no orders from no one."

"He meets up with you often? Where do you both meet up every week?"

"Yes, the alleyway behind the store. It's a trail that leads to the woods but I guess that where he hides out. He meets me halfway out that alleyway."

Jenna and Mark were delightfully flustered about now. They'd made sure to search for Amy and Louis everywhere-except. Except the woods. And that's of course, the place to go after, after all.

"Look, I don't know what's going on around here but I just know Louis is guilty for something here and just please, catch him already."

A desperate and helpless sounding Christopher's words were now of grave importance to Jenna.

"When do you usually meet up with him?"

"Usually Wednesdays. He calls around Mondays or Tuesdays to get the things he needs. Then at Tuesday evenings again to make sure I'd show up with the things the next day."

"So, if he calls you today, you'd meet him tomorrow, right?"

Just as Mark asked that question, Christopher's phone rings.

It is Louis calling.

Jenna instructs Christopher to pick up the call and act normal and agree to meet up the next day.

Christopher being the errand boy who's willing to risk it all and expose Louis, for a good deal that maybe spares him, did exactly as he was told. He didn't voluntarily get into this mess anyways - or so he says. With that being said, everyone prepared themselves to take down Louis.

DAY 24 since Amy

The day has finally come. They were at a pace to finally catch their main suspect in the case. Everyone in position. Ready to go in for the action. Everything was set in play.

Instructing him on how to move through his ear piece, Jenna was right behind Christopher as he approached the alleyway towards Louis.

There was no one in sight so far. They waited patiently anyways.

After a moment's time, someone was walking towards Christopher from the woods. Jenna couldn't make out who it was from her position, and just then, an officer in a different position says,

"Identity confirmed, that's the suspect."

CHAPTER III

Cameras flashing, people shouting, officers all around trying to get a hold of the chaos, Jenna and Mark make the grand entry to the station with a handcuffed Louis.

The news of his arrest seemed to have reached further than the faraway lands and ears of way too many ear biting journalists.

'A few days ago, no news of missing girls or Amy was of catch to any reporter… all of a sudden, how'd this become the talk of the town?'

Jenna and Mark's thoughts once again telepathically crossed one another.

Trying to get a proper hold of the situation, Jenna and Mark tried to take in Louis to the station through the crowd somehow, but the crowd started to take matters into their own hands.

"Where's Amy?" "Did you kidnap your own stepdaughter Mr. Smith?" "Is she still alive?"

Questions and interrogations were taking place amidst all the pushing and crowding as if it was a free consultation as is.

Escorting Louis into the interrogation room was yet another task for them again coz' awaiting them inside the station was another crowd with every detective and officer present there and the chief!

They entered and asked the duty cops to take Louis into the interrogation room, while Jenna and Mark decided to go to the chief themselves to know what exactly was happening. The chief on the other hand was trying his best to slip out of their conversation, knowing he crossed the line on this one.

"Chief, it's not like we've closed the case or got anything solid! How could you get the media involved right now? Who's going to manage all of that while we've got a possible culprit in our hands?"

"Hey now, why don't you both calm down? You have your guy- NAIL HIM! About all that outside, leave that to me. That's only to add on to all the good we have been doing alright. It was about time we bring in some good name to this place and our work- your work. So, pay less attention to that and go do your damn jobs!!"

The chief left a very annoyed Jenna and Mark in middle of their conversation and expected all to be done soon, as in the case's status.

With even more frustration added onto their minds, Jen and Mark decided to cool off their minds before going in and questioning Louis.

Just as they were headed in, Mark stopped and looked around. Jenna stopped after him and asked what he was looking for.

"Nothing... it's just... even if the news wasn't out.. . Linda's supposed to be here. I don't see her anywhere though."

Jenna noticed it after Mark pointing it out too.

"Maybe she don't wana face her husband who's in custody for the possible kidnapping of her daughter..."

With Jenna's convincing reply, both of them enter the room.

Louis was sitting there, staring at them. Something about

his glare did not feel right though. He didn't look scared or surprised or anything of that sort. It was as if he already prepared himself for this. He looked as if he had it all planned.

In contrast to Christopher's first impression, Louis was not going for an all-calm-but-confident deceiving composure, but for a perfectly-prepared-for-anything-you-throw-at-me composure.

Jenna sat down, her eyes still fixed on him. Mark sat beside her and started to get his notes and everything ready. Louis then stared at Mark prepping the laptop and smirked.

"Anything that amuses you here, Mr. Smith?" Jenna asked.

"Ooh. Mr. Smith? Please. It's Louis, miss-"

He stopped, expecting a name from Jen. But she remained silent with a cold attitude towards him.

"Alright. Detective it is. Amusing you ask? Huh. What really amuses me is what I am doing here with my hands cuffed when the person I was supposedly meeting is freely walking about- out there."

Mark asked, with a surprised look on his face, *"Excuse me?"*

Even though they already predicted Louis to be cunning enough to turn it all on Christopher for giving him in and uncooperative in the first place, they didn't expect him to start his act this soon.

"Yes detective. I am wondering what it is that you both have on me that might've been fed to you by that pretty boy Chris, which by the way could be complete nonsense. And even if it's not, whatever it is, he should be locked in for it before me!"

"Mr. Smith...Louis- are you trying to say you have done nothing wrong? Or that you have done something that accompanies Christopher?"

"Oh... I see how this works. Why don't you detectives tell me what I did that's illegal or why I'm here in the first place

and I'll let you know if it's true or not."

Squirming around to find out exactly how much Jenna and Mark knows, Louis kept on going on unbothered by Mark's questions.

"Let's not pretend to play games now, Louis. You know why you are in here. Why don't you start by telling us where Amy is?"

Mark didn't want to waste any more time and decided to jump start the session.

Unfazed by Mark's direct question, Louis acting out a shocked face, mockingly asked back,

"Amy? My sweet daughter? What about her? Is she not home?"

Both Jenna and Mark expected Louis to be oblivious, but having him test their patience, they kind of prepared their mind to stay put… for they knew they were in for a long ride.

Jenna decided to take a different approach by playing along with him.

"Why don't we start small then? Where have you been since May 8th?"

"Oh, 8th? Home? I guess? I don't remember for sure but I guess I was probably home. Why don't you ask Linda? She'd know for sure."

"We did and you were not home. You have been off the grid with no one seeing you or having any type of contact with you. Except for Christopher of course. The last sighting of you was at the store, right beside Christopher. Now, where'd you go after leaving the store? The woods through the alleyway behind the store perhaps?"

Jenna had her questions incoming with her eyebrow raised and a wicked smile. Louis on the other hand, seemed perfectly fine even after seeing the camera footage from the store. It was as if he knew they had nothing of solid proof incriminating him or isn't going to find any soon.

It looked like he was just there trying to buy time till his 48 hours were up to leave. Anyways, without any change in his tone, he replied,

"Oh, was that the day I vanished into the woods? Ha! I didn't keep track of it- sorry! Yea, I've been in the nature's nest for a while... guess people found it hard to reach me after all!"

"Not everyone at least. Why did you have Christopher buy you these supplies every week? Anyone hurt that you've been looking after maybe? Anyone you don't wana disclose?"

Mark didn't take any chance when it came to questioning him and made sure to bring up Amy's name in any chance possible.

Louis hesitated for a moment, sat up straight and looked at Mark with a faint smile.

"Come on now, I only had him buy me some water and stuff to look after myself in the woods of course. That's the least he should be doing for me to keep my mouth shut!"

"Your mouth shut? Did Christopher do something to you that you'd like to tell us?"

"Well, now that I think about it, it's actually a bit more than something. Where is he anyway? You didn't let that Chris boy walk now, did you?"

Louis kept bringing it all back to Christopher just as Jenna and Mark predicted.

"Mr. Smith, why don't you try harder to prove your innocence and try a little less to turn our attention to someone else?"

Jenna was not going to go for the he said- she said scenario and decided to get him straight.

"Wow detective. There's nothing for me to prove you see... I'm innocent and you can't prove am guilty of something I haven't done! And also, if it's coming off like am trying to turn

your attention somewhere else, that's because it should be!"

Jenna sighed and got up to take a breather knowing this conversation isn't going anywhere. Mark followed right behind.

Going over on how to break him, Mark suggests to go along with Louis.

"Either way, one of them or both of them is guilty of something. Why don't we play along and let them draw the straws for each other. Christopher's booked in anyway, we can cross examine them as we'd like once we get something useful out of Louis."

Jenna agreed and decided to go with Mark's strategy. With a new game plan, they both enter the interrogation room once again.

"Ok Louis, let's get something straight here. You are our top suspect to have done anything with Amy who has been missing for 24 days. That's why you are in here! You could either cooperate to help us find her or you could choose your life sentence. You see... we've already got plenty of leverage to lock you up from Christopher. So if you think you're getting away with anything or gona walk out from here as a free man- you are wrong."

With an affirmative smirk mocking him, Jenna made it clear to Louis that it's either get caught talking or get caught hiding.

Louis was startled. He didn't know exactly what was in Jenna and Mark's hands or exactly how much Christopher did talk. All he thought of doing was stalling but now that things have changed, he decided to take measures too.

"So tell me detective... it's anybody's words against mine? I mean, isn't there something called fact checking or background check of some kind...before blindly believing anything someone say? How much of this Chris person do you know actually?"

Jenna and Mark had him right where they wanted him.

"Why don't you enlighten us if you know so much about Christopher?"

Mark put out the bait.

"How'd you meet Christopher, Louis?"

Jenna set the bait in place.

"A great question finally!"

Louis' eyes sparkled. He sat up straight with a smile and started to speak again,

"Now, you're taking the word of the guy who I met through the perfect act- that being him trying to get all handsy with Amy and also her friend- Stella something. I saw them both trying to stop him or whatever and gave him a piece of my mind! That's how I first met him. Yea. Ever since, he's been dead scared of me"

"Louis… you're telling us, Christopher was misbehaving with Stella and Amy?"

"Ooh, misbehaving- pretty word. But yea, if that explains it, yes."

"You're sure of what you saw? You're not reading anything more to it or anything-coz from what we gather, Christopher and Stella were in a relationship."

"Hah! Where did you gather that from?!"

"Did Stella tell you otherwise?"

Jenna's question made Louis stumble for a moment, but he kept going,

"Why should she? Even if anything did go on with them, Amy had no reason to be involved, now did she? But they were always together. And it was as if Amy was only there for Stella- as some kind of protection against this Chris boy or something. Funny, really. How they used to be around him. But yea, I figured they'd find their way out on their own so I didn't bother much about it."

"You're telling us, your stepdaughter and her teenage friend could have been abused by a person that you saw in such a situation yourself, and you didn't care to... I don't know... help them? Rescue them?"

"Whoa, rescue them? They were not in danger now detective. They had each other. They looked fine too. If they could take care of each other, why should I interfere?"

Jenna and Mark were both being tested by their patience so hard. However, they decide to keep going.

"You literally mentioned how Amy was trying to protect Stella a few seconds ago."

"Oh yea, that would be true too."

Louis had his mouth run off with a carefree attitude. Jen just didn't understand how he was so calm and reckless with his words and actions too.

They got out of the room once again. Feeling all huffed up and frustrated, Jen and Mark didn't want to go back empty handed. They called the cops on site for the search party in the woods to know if they had any luck with anything.

An urgently cut off call due to the restless K-9 running around only added onto Jenna's pile of stress.

That's when it hit Jen. All she had to was make Louis think they found something from the woods. After all, trying a new strategy couldn't harm them in anyway as long as they made sure not to lie about anything.

With a new strategy all set, Jenna and Mark is back in the interrogation room with Louis smirking at them. They sat across him and began their presumably last and final act.

"So Louis, did you cover everything about Christopher from your side? If not, I'd suggest you to hurry coz' we've got plenty of other stuff to take care of."

A slightly bothered Louis on the sudden change of Jenna's and Mark's attitude, didn't know what was going on. As prepared as he was or as he had looked, he didn't think far enough for the search going on in the woods.

"Am sorry detective, I thought you guys brought me in here... you know... not the other way around... aren't I supposed to be the one who wants to leave whenever?"

Mark laughed at Louis' statement.

"Wow, Louis- now you. are. one. funny. guy. Damn!"

"There's nothing to laugh about in what I said."

"Is that what you think? You were serious? Oh man, my bad. Well, I guess now you know the answer to your question."

"Is this the new strategy then? Play dumb and mock me in the off chance of trying to get something out of me?"

They were starting to get to Louis and he knew it.

"Hey now, there's no strategy. I feel like you don't have a hang of what's happening here. We don't need to break you, Louis. We've already got plenty of what we needed from the woods."

That struck Louis. His eyes widened, staring at Jenna. He finally was shook.

What he thought he'd achieve- was all over in his eyes. All the game pieces he arranged and managed to play… only to have forgotten about the most important one.

A startled and speechless Louis gave the final key to Jenna and Mark. The woods. Amy is in the woods.

Trying to hold in their actual expression towards the critical piece of information they just got on their hands, Jenna gets out to inform the cops on site that Amy's there somewhere. Mark gets up to leave too and says,

"Well, thank you for your time Louis. Let's meet again soon, shall we?"

Accepting his defeat, he decides to clutch on to his last minute measures. He knew he was going down anyway but he had to make sure to get something out of it- some kind of deal.

If he was going to be sentenced for his crimes, he'd rather split it in half by sharing the blame on someone instead of facing it all on his own… so he catches up to speed and decides to act accordingly.

Jenna was basically out the door when Louis suddenly got up.

"Wait-"

She turned back and looked at Mark all confused. They didn't expect Louis to break at all, so Louis calling them back was not part of their plan.

Jenna texted the officers at the site and got back in the room along with Mark to hear what he has to say.

"It was not me alright. Not alone. He was there too. Christopher. You can ask her yourself. She would say the same too."

Jenna and Mark remained silent, trying to contain their very confused minds to themselves because they didn't know what he was talking about. But they couldn't let him know that. Not when they had him possibly confessing to something they were about to find.

Jenna starts connecting the dots. Milinca's statement. Stella's disappearance. Louis' abusive nature that Christopher described. Christopher's behavior that Louis described. It all made sense.

Without saying a word, Jenna opens the door, walks out slowly, a thousand emotions all raging on at once inside her. Mark followed her right behind.

As she tries to walk out of the station, she trips… Mark held her and saw how she was light headed and about to lose consciousness.

"Hey Jen... Jen... are you ok?"

Mark's voice was echoing in Jenna's head but she couldn't reply. All she could think about was of Amy and Stella. The poor girls.

In a moment of weakness, Jenna was down helpless and finally realizing how the case had got to her. But as Mark's voice kept echoing in her subconscious mind, she manages to get out of her own head.

Trying to recover quickly from her panic attack, Jenna with a heavy deep breath, got back on her feet.

"Ca... call them... they're... they are in need of medical attention. Get an ambulance there- quick."

"Wait, what? Jen, who is in need of medical attention? Are you ok? Can you stand on your own?"

Mark was worried more about his Jenna to try and take orders from her about others.

"THE GIRLS MARK! THE GIRLS! It's possible they were raped by those vicious monsters in there, so GET THEM THE HELP THEY NEED!"

Both Jenna and Mark stood there staring at each other with much tension rising by the second. Jenna's phone kept ringing but she couldn't pay attention to it with what was going through at that moment.

Mark got a call then. It was from the officers at site. He answered the call, seeing as to how he was only listening, Jen assumed they found Amy. But he wasn't asking about her condition or asking for the ambulance that Jenna told him to get. He was just there, listening to the call, staring at Jenna, all silent.

She got restless and asked Mark why he wasn't saying anything. He didn't speak a word still.

"What's wrong with you Mark? Get her to the goddamn hospital already if her condition is that bad. Tell them to make sure she's safe!!"

A completely silent and still Mark made Jenna furious. Trying to take the phone from him, Jenna came close to him about to snatch his phone away. He put his hands down. He looked at Jen and said,

"They found her. They found Amy."

"Yea, I got that. Now ask them about her condition and send her to the hospital with a female offi-"

Cutting off Jen, Mark said- "Buried."

Jenna stopped. Her legs froze to the ground. Her hands stuck in position. She wanted to believe she just misheard something. She wanted to make sure Amy was alright. She wanted to go meet her herself. She wanted to deliver the good news of finding her daughter to Linda herself.

Jenna desperately hoped Mark would just correct himself and speak again.

She stood there, ice cold, motionless, staring at Mark, desperately holding back tears and herself from breaking down, waiting for him to finish his sentence.

"They found her body buried."

CHAPTER IV

After 24 days of devastating hunt for Amy, Jenna and Mark walk into the final steps of meeting her. Except, they had imagined this scenario under different circumstances.

As they are escorted by the other officers through a long trail into the woods, a hundred thoughts cross their mind. Any detective should be prepared for the worst case scenario but with all the effort, time and days they spent on this one, both of them hoped for a different ending.

They get closer to a crowd of people. A group of cops holding off a swarm of reporters and cameras in the side, was not a sight that brought ease into Jenna and Mark's minds at the moment too.

They walk in to the crowd, gets past all the chaos and in front lies a covered body.

Jenna looked around trying to analyze what had happened. The dug out grave looked rather fresh and not from too long ago.

There was a bunker of some sort a few meters away from the grave. That seemed to be Louis' hideout after all. Quite mysterious and well hidden, deep in the forest. No wonder why he thought he had all the time in the world before they could catch on.

Jenna with a sunken heart, didn't want to examine the body first. She walked away and straight into the bunker that looked pretty rusty.

Everything was already being examined and tested by the forensic team on the site, but she made her way through to see for herself.

"This old rusty beat up and used camper van that was seemingly transformed into a bunker, was where Amy was. This was where we couldn't find her. This was where Louis hid her from us for the past many weeks. This is where it all ends?"

Jenna's thoughts started to pile on once again.

She looked around and saw blood stains everywhere. Nail scraped marks were found in all kinds of nook and corner too. Jenna was beyond disgusted and haunted thinking of what Amy went through in this place.

As she looks around, Mark calls out for her. Slightly relieved to leave that place of horror, Jenna walks out of the bunker towards Mark who was standing in front of the coroner's van.

"Jen, you need to see this."

He opened the van's door to show something to Jenna.

"Two bodies? Why is there another body?"

"They found another body during the search a bit far from here. They identified the body as well"

Jenna looked at Mark now, she knew it wasn't good news she was about to hear. As destroyed as she was at the moment, Jenna tried to keep herself from exploding and decided to take up the little courage left in her to accept whatever she was about to hear.

Mark on the other hand could read Jenna like an open book. He hesitated to speak anything at all. But he finally said,

"It's Stella."

Jenna was shook to her core. She immediately got into the van and pulled the sheets over to see the faces of the bodies for herself, coz' she didn't want to take someone else's word for it.

She pulled the sheets off only to be horrified by what lied in front of her. She could surprisingly identify Amy but all the scratches, wounds and her swollen face made it almost impossible.

Stella's body on the other hand was nearly rotten to be almost completely unrecognizable. The only way the cops on the site assumed it to be Stella is as of her half deteriorated clothes and other belongings identified on the body.

Following her sudden spur of the moment act, regrets followed.

The stench of rotten bodies. The unrecognizably deteriorated face of Stella. A beaten to a pulp, eyes almost scourged out, blood covered face of Amy. Everything was way more than anything Jenna was prepared for. She couldn't break down though. Not with all of the eyes present on the situation.

A mortified Jenna who could barely move or breath, managed to get off the coroner's van and slowly started to walk away from all the chaos. Trying to get away from all the people to catch her breath again, she slowly walked away from the scene. Mark followed a clearly unstable Jenna.

Jenna managed to walk on her own for a bit, but as her head started to spin with a next panic attack coming in, she stopped. Mark held her seeing as to how she was about to fall. She sat down, trying to calm down. Mark sat down beside her.

As they sat there, in middle of the forest, all silent, with a million questions and emotions exploding inside them, tears started to flow down Jenna's face. She didn't want Mark to see her cry but she couldn't hold it in anymore.

They both share a soft vulnerable moment with each other consoling one another by just their presence. They slowly start to realize the next steps they'll have to take to bring an end to this. With every passing second, Heavy thoughts start to consume them again. Mark finally broke the silence,

"So when should we meet Linda?"

Jenna with puffed up eyes looked at Mark with an exhausted expression. Trying to bring her mood back up, he continues,

"Come on Jen, we just can't let go of it all now. We should at least give Linda what we can, justice for her daughter I mean. Let's get those monsters locked in once and for all!"

That got her attention. The fire inside Jen that was slightly fading away just got the fuel it needed. She got up and realized what she had to do. She got Mark up too and started to head back to the station to make sure things were being handled exactly as it should've been in the first place.

Back at the station, it was no Greenland and peace. The chief drew his straw with the media and knew he made a big mistake by his own actions. The press was all over the station and demanded updates about the case every minute.

Jenna and Mark enter the station and head straight to the holding cell to get to Christopher first. She paid no attention to all the reporters or the chief who was anxiously waiting for the lead detectives of the case to brief them.

Mark had a word with the chief and decided that they would stay out of all the media talk and let the chief handle it all on his own. Meanwhile, they got Christopher into another interrogation room.

Christopher was baffled. He didn't understand what was going on.

"Mr. Christopher Lynn, here's a rundown of today's events. At 9:18 am, we set up the meeting with you and Louis Smith. After the confrontation, we returned to the station by 10 am, with both you Christopher and Louis. It was in between our interrogation with Louis, that we were called out of station for an emergency. At about 3 in the afternoon we were on site,

in the woods. We found Amy."

"You did? Wow. Ok. Is she fine? Is she ok? Louis had her all this time?"

"We got Stella too."

Mark noted how Christopher's expression completely changed after he revealed Stella was found too.

"Ste…Stella? Umm… they were both together? Louis had them? Umm… is she ok? Where…. What… where are they now?"

Jenna had all her anger and frustration building up inside her. She could see how Christopher was mumbling for words trying to act a fool in front of them as it was clearly unexpected.

With the coldest attitude ever, Jen replied to Christopher's question,

"Both Amy and Stella are probably at the coroner's right about now."

"Wait what? W… Wh… What… why… "

For a second, Jenna and Mark were almost convinced that he was genuinely surprised to hear it. But they didn't let their minds get twisted and chose to get both Louis and Christopher convicted no matter what. For they were both guilty of something. They just had to find what it was they were individually guilty of.

At this point, Jenna and Mark were just waiting for the coroner's report to make their arrests and close the case. While waiting for the report, they decided to have a go at both Christopher and Louis to see if they would actually confess to their crimes.

Now that Mark and Jen could guess how they were not going to easily confess their way out, they decided to let them know that the eventual fate awaiting them is prison. But if they were to cooperate and speak up for their crimes, they might get a better deal in reducing their time there.

"So the choice is yours, Christopher. I'd advise you to make a wise one provided that you don't have a lot of options either way."

Mark's words were echoing in Christopher's head. This was his last stand. After hesitating for a while, he decided to give in. He finally chose to take the deal.

"First of all, I want to make it clear. I did not take part in it. I... I did not do it-"

"Do what? Murder? Why don't you start by telling us everything you know?"

"It was all coz of Stella alright. She was the one who came onto me. I mean, we were in a relationship with mutual interests. But that's... that's how the problems started. Amy was getting in between us more often and Stella was somehow not bothered at all. Most times, it was as if I was third wheeling in my own date you know! That's why I decided to break it off with Stella! She wasn't happy but I chose to leave her anyway. Especially with what happened with Louis and stuff. I was just way over it. Didn't want to be part of any of it. Yea... for a few days... or weeks... everything was cool. But she reached out. You know. Like I said before... Stella called."

His voice slowly started to change tone. It was clear to Jen how he was hesitating to talk trying to hide something.

"Christopher, I guess it's time for you to realize the situation you are in right now. No good is going to come with you hiding stuff from us. We have told you before and we'll tell you again. Whatever it is, we'll find it in a matter of time. So it is us finding it out from you or finding it out from someone else. Why don't you save yourself some time and tell us already?"

Jenna calmly set Christopher's mind on fire.

He looked at Jenna, then Mark and then faced down. Right then, under his breath he whispered,

"She was pregnant."

Jenna thought she had seen everything that could haunt her by discovering Amy's and Stella's bodies. But things left for her to hear before closing this case was definitely going to leave her soul scarred.

She got up and left the room. Mark followed her.

Trying to piece her mind together to avoid another episode of a meltdown, Jenna paced through the station. She finally calmed down and looked at the time. It was going to be six and she couldn't let the autopsy report to be delayed so she personally asked the coroner to do what it takes despite the clock.

The entire town wanted justice for these girls that they misjudged to be runaways when in reality they were tortured to death.

Due to their delayed pity and responsibility towards the girls, without a second of doubt, everything was being taken care of. So it didn't take a lot to convince the medical examiners too.

Just as she ended the call and turned to Mark who was behind her… A familiar voice of another person was heard. Linda. She was standing in front of them, pale as a white sheet, with eyes that had obviously gone through a lot. She didn't speak a word. She just stood there in silence, staring into a blank space between Mark and Jenna.

Mark, usually the person to know how to act according to the situation around Linda, was also baffled and at a loss of words.

The three stood there, not knowing what to do or how to start the conversation.

Jenna then approached Linda and slightly placed her hand on Linda's shoulder. She looked at Jen after being called. Slowly regaining consciousness back to reality, she started to have tears in her eyes, while staring at Jenna.

Call it a twisted fate or just the worst turn of events, the next interrogation was about to take place and Louis was being escorted out of the holding cell into the interrogation room. His voice amidst the chaos in the station stood out the most.

Jenna, immediately reading Linda's expression, tried to distract her by asking her to come with Jen to take a seat somewhere else. Ignoring Jenna's voice, Linda slowly turned towards the source of his sound. Louis was caught off guard when he noticed Linda amidst the crowd too. But, instantly, he smirked.

Louis was now wickedly smiling at Linda, knowing she was in pain of what he did to her.

Linda, who was barely standing on her own, helplessly started to scream. Her cry was so real that anyone nearby could feel her pain too.

She then ran towards Louis, grabbed him by his collars and started screaming more. Jenna, Mark and other officers came to the rescue and separated the two.

The astonishing sight for everyone present there was a handcuffed Louis standing there with a smile even after being attacked by Linda. Jenna asked the cops to take him away.

They stayed back with a broken Linda, who was now weeping on her knees.

Everybody at the station was stuck for a moment, stayed put, not a single sound. Every officer, criminal and every person there, just stood frozen, unable to react to the painful cry of a deeply heartbroken mother.

Slowly, trying to get a hold of Linda, Mark approaches and takes her by the hands to a corner where there were less eyes on her. Jenna and Mark stood by her side till she came to a point where she could lift her head up and open her eyes again. She didn't speak a word though.

She looked up at Jenna, with her hands clutched on her chest, almost as if she was trying to keep herself alive coz' her heart could give up any second. No words spoken but a lot of emotions conveyed to one another by just looking at each other.

Jen then went on her knees in front of Linda, held her trembling hands on her lap and in a comforting reassuring tone said,

"We will make sure whoever was behind Amy, will never walk free again. I will make sure that wherever she is, she'll finally get the justice she deserves. You hang in there Linda. Don't give up just yet."

Hearing Jenna, Linda nodded along but couldn't help but tear up again.

Just then, another officer walked in and announced that Stella's parents were looking for them setting a havoc of their own.

After handling a devastated Linda and Stella's frustratingly heartbroken parents, Jenna and Mark returned to Christopher to finish what they started.

A guilty looking ashamed Christopher looked at Jenna and Mark as they entered but couldn't meet their eyes. He slowly turned his head away from them and down to his feet again.

Jenna was beyond disgusted at this point. She wanted to settle all this and send these monsters to the very cage they deserve and be treated for what they are- ruthless. Vicious. Monsters.

"Let's continue Christopher. Now where were we?"

He didn't respond to Mark and stayed put, still staring at his feet, apparently riddled by his own supposed guilty consciousness.

"What did you do after finding out Stella was pregnant, Christopher?"

Mark's question made him look up again. Speechless, he just stared at Mark for a while and losing their patience, Jenna and Mark decided to trigger him,

"Look, you can play dumb as long as you want, we will get our answers from Louis if not from you. So. You. Take your time."

Christopher's eyebrows furrowed. Raising his voice bit by bit,

"Louis will give you answers?? Him? He will-"

Christopher was having an outburst but trying to keep himself under control.

How he was trying to control his anger was obvious and suspicious. It was as if he was trying to make sure to hide his anger and what he was actually capable of.

Stating the obvious, Jenna and Mark were not blind to his actions and just waited for him to complete his act.

He calmed down and with a lighter tone, started to speak again.

"Sorry I lost it for a second. Don't really appreciate bringing Louis into this every time alright! He's the reason I am in this mess in the first place!"

"Louis? I thought you were saying it was Stella's fault."

Christopher was once again holding back, looking at Jenna as she mocked him.

"Yes detective. Stella is the reason I got involved but the reason I am sitting here in front of you right now is because of Louis. If he held back his psychotic reactions a little, I wouldn't be here at all. And who knows, maybe both Stella and Amy would still be alive too!"

"Are you saying he murdered Stella and Amy?"

Christopher took a second, sat up straight in a more relaxed form. Feeling all pleased, he thought he had them right where he intended in the first place.

"I thought that was a given now that you have found their bodies from his place or whatever, isn't it obvious already?"

Jenna had a flash of what she experienced in the crime

scene. She could see their faces infront of her. She had the terror in her eyes. She started to freeze up again. Mark caught that from the side of his eye. He let her calm down by holding her hand under the desk and making her return to reality.

Frustrated with a sudden turn to a horrific sight, Jenna bursts out at Christopher.

"Is that all Christopher? You are gona say it was all him and you had nothing to do with any of it? Really? You seriously expect us to take your word for this?"

A sudden outburst from Jenna shocked and surprised Christopher. Enough to make him start talking in fear. He whispered,

"I didn't say that"

Christopher was back to looking guilty and once again stared at his feet.

After a moment of silence, he continued to talk under his breath,

"She did meet me... that day... at the store. She wanted to tell me about it. She wanted me to take care of it... like as if I could!"

"The pregnancy, you mean?"

"Yes... it was like she was threatening me out of nowhere with something I was obviously not prepared for. Like I didn't know how to react... so... so we did have an argument of sorts. You know. We were trying to figure it out but things were so out of hand. So one thing lead to another and... I mean... she pushed me... and I just reacted like-"

"The disagreement got physical?"

"No, I mean... not physical like that... but... we were just harsh with each other."

"What happened next?"

Christopher stumbled for words as Jen asked about what came next. He was hesitating and started to break a sweat trying to make up something. Jenna, catching on quick, once again reminded him of how he was only digging his own pit deeper with every lie he gave.

Reminded of his eventual fate, he finally gave in.

"She passed out. She was down alright. Didn't wake up even after I called her and all. That's when Louis came in. He was at the store and had been watching from afar... like a creep... He said he saw everything and knew about the pregnancy. He was getting all cocky and started to beat me up. He kept going on about useless things and kicking me till I passed out. When I woke up, she wasn't there. So wasn't he. I thought she'd gone home or something. I seriously did. I thought she'd take care of it on her own without her parents knowing and stuff...but... she just vanished. At first, I thought she had gone somewhere silent to settle matters. She wasn't picking my calls or texts, then again... I just figured she cut off all contact with me to just block me out of her life or something. But then yea, after a while... Louis' calls and threats started. I did think Stella was behind it but as Louis was involved, I'd reckoned Amy was in on it too. That's when I decided to meet up with Amy."

Jenna was surprised to hear that. Christopher meeting Amy after Stella's disappearance was a first.

She didn't know if everything Christopher was saying could be trusted but she decided to hear him out anyway.

"You met Amy then? When was this?"

"I don't know, maybe like the beginning of May? Someday then I guess. But yea I decided to meet her and see what their deal was... Surprisingly, she had no idea!"

Christopher's words seemed to be genuine with how he was expressing them. Mark was on the fence on being swayed by his words however. Never the less, he resumed his part of the story.

"She was completely shocked to see me and asked me

about Stella! It was as if she never spoke to Stella at all. When I mentioned about Stella being pregnant and all, Amy was just... a complete mess. She was like trying Stella on her phone or something but there was no answer. I asked her when was the last time they spoke and apparently they were in a spat themselves coz Amy didn't want her meeting me in the first place. She didn't know about Stella's need to meet me and thought it was about getting back together or something which she clearly opposed. She didn't know about a single thing for that long and was panicking like something bad had happened to Stella. She was about to leave until I told her about Louis being there... overhearing us and stuff. She was shocked again to hear that. She asked if I saw Stella leaving or something and since I was passed out at that time I didn't know what happened after... which only made Amy mad and she like stormed off! I tried calling her after that, she never picked up. I even waited around the school looking for her but she wasn't there. So I thought she might've gone to where Stella was hiding and all. But... Louis...you know... he just..."

Jenna just wanted to go over this with Louis and try to confirm as much as possible. She rushed Christopher to finish faster because she didn't have the heart to listen to any more of their made up self-saving stories.

"Yea. Umm... he didn't leave me. The calls and the threats kept coming every now and then. So I met him and confronted him. He just did the usual and beat me up till I passed out again. Except this time, before I passed out... he said something about Stella. Something about me going to jail for her or something. That's when I knew. That's when I started helping him out. I didn't want to end up... like her..."

"You are saying you knew something happened to Stella and chose to stay silent?"

"I didn't want to end up dead too! It's not like I did something wrong trying not to get killed!! I didn't kill anyone now... DID I?"

Jenna and Mark were perplexed on how confident Christopher was trying to prove he did nothing wrong or so he believed. They couldn't tell if he was acting naïve or just completely consumed by himself.

Mark was losing trust in him by every passing minute by how his personality kept changing. Jenna never had any in the first place so they decide to move on and see if he had anything more to say so Jenna asked,

"That was the last time you ever saw or heard from Amy then? The day you met her?"

"Yea. After that, she vanished too. But I swear. I really didn't know anything about her. I didn't know Louis had her. I really just found out about her being involved in this at all when you guys informed me about her being missing and stuff!"

After a surprising but a disappointing interrogation with Christopher, Jenna and Mark were headed towards Louis.

They walked towards the room he was being held in with a heavy heart, coz' they didn't know what to expect after how he reacted to Linda.

They opened the door and as they walked in, Louis was staring at them with a wicked smile.

"Well, well, well. Finally here. we. are."

Louis' opening statement in itself with his expression was shockingly absurd. Jenna and Mark were both flabbergasted. It was as if he had the control over the room and didn't care about any consequences for his actions.

No game plan or strategies were set walking in and after witnessing him being his true self, Jenna and Mark didn't know how to approach this at all.

They sat down without saying a word and just stared down at Louis waiting for him to start talking on his own.

"What's with this heavy feeling that you guys have brought

in with yourselves detectives?!! Come on now... take a chill pill!!"

Sitting in front of a psychopath was not in Jenna's to do list for the day but she put through it to get some kind of closure.

To stop him from enjoying his spotlight a bit too much, she started asking questions.

"Tell us Louis. Why did you do it?"

"Do what?"

The high pitched reply mocking them only raised their anger even more.

"You think this is funny? Everything that you've done is funny? Going to prison for murder charges is funny to you?"

A smiling Louis suddenly changed his expression. He looked a bit surprised and tried to play it off by chuckling nervously. He looked at Jenna and then at Mark and asked

"Murder? Well now, who died?"

Jenna and Mark's patience was long gone seeing how Louis was acting.

Mark was the one who blasted in anger this time. He stood up, hit the desk with both his hands and shouted

"What do you think you are playing at? Huh? If you think you're getting away with anything, oh you are going down. I will make sure of it myself!"

Now, putting on a whole different slightly deranged face, Louis stood up and started speaking in a lower tone

"Excuse me detective, but let's not call in for more than what's done. No one's dead and no one is going in for any false murder charges alright!"

Jenna clenched her fist so hard, trying to control her emotions and herself from going over the desk and hitting Louis to a point where he doesn't reckon to wake up again.

A completely frustrated Jenna took over,

"Are you really trying to claim you have nothing to do with the murder of Amy and Stella?"

Louis chuckled again. He seemed to be thinking Jenna and Mark were joking or lying for some reason. He then realized how both Jenna and Mark were holding themselves back from attacking him.

Nervously looking back and forth between them, he whispered

"She's dead?"

He slowly sat back down as if accepting a defeat he didn't see coming. Somehow, his reaction seemed convincingly surprised to Jenna and Mark.

He turned his head towards them and whispered again,

"But I made sure she was breathing..."

Jenna's eyebrows raised with more patience tested,

"Do you expect us to be grateful to you for that?"

He looked up at her and smiled again. He was back to being cocky and somehow decided to play it cool even if he was going to prison for murder.

Trying to hold Jenna back from crushing Louis, Mark stepped in,

"You are going to prison for life. Have fun in there. Double homicide will easily give you your dream life of course! So hang in there."

Once again, getting up with a surprised face, Louis put on his next act...

"Whoa, whoa, double? Am sorry what? Is this some kind of one plus one deal am getting for free or something? What double?"

Mark gave him a warning before they were about to leave the room,

"You seriously want us to hit you or something? Really?"

"Is it Stella you guys are talking about? The friend? Why would I have anything to do with her? Didn't you detectives already establish her relationship with that Chris boy? I told you I wasn't alone in any of this!"

Jenna and Mark were more than done with how both Christopher and Louis were playing them!

They both looked at each other and sighed. They were about to leave not wanting to hear any more of all this bickering.

A desperate Louis, however, couldn't take the fall for everything. He started speaking in a rushed out of breath voice,

"Hey... hey... listen alright. You don't need to take my word for it alright. Don't you guys have some kind of way to find out like the time of death or something... the autopsy! Yea! You guys can know when someone died from that... right. If you look at your records too... the last day Stella was seen was at the store, with Christopher. I walked in on it myself. How he was hitting her and stuff. She passed out and that's it. She died on the spot alright. He hit her head pretty hard with something and I walked in on that. If you look at the dates and all, everything will match for sure!"

Now this turn of tables was unexpectedly expected. But how half and half of each other's stories matched coincidentally was as if it was all pre-planned. It was as if both of them managed to have a clear cut story to blame the other and spare themselves.

Tempted to hear the rest of what he had to say to see the picture he painted, Jenna and Mark decided to stay.

Judging their expressions, Louis started to speak again,

"Well yea, he was the one who literally killed someone, so you should be getting him! Not me!"

Trying to let him in on the other side of the story, Mark said,

"According to Christopher however, you walked in on them fighting and beat him up until he passed out. And once he woke up, you were gone. And so was Stella."

"Wow. You believe that? How dumb is it for me to just walk away with a dead body? Why would I do that?"

"Why don't you tell us?"

Trying to grasp the situation, Louis decides to act quickly despite the triggering replies from Mark.

"Ok here's what really happened. So I did walk in on them right. She was lying there. Not moving and stuff. I wanted to make sure if she was alive and once I saw how she wasn't breathing, I decided to walk away. But HE! He stopped me! He caught me and started going nuts on how to help him and stuff! I did push him off and scare him a little, but nothing too serious! That's when he showed me the photos he had of my stash and stuff. I took his phone and broke it at an instant but he claimed to still have it saved somewhere and was gona use it against me to the cops if I didn't help him! So yea, I did help him cover up. That's all. Ok? That's all I did to that friend."

"That's all you did? Really? Like do you really need an answer to that?"

Jenna and Mark were not so surprised by the he-said-she-said scenario they were in right now. They decided to leave it all to the final verdict from the autopsy report.

As they approached towards the door to leave the room, Jenna turned back and asked a final question.

"If you did help cover up Stella in one place... why did you choose to bury Amy right in front of your hideout?"

Louis stood up at Jenna's revelation. With his eyes wide open, he raised his voice,

"WHAT? Buried whom?"

His reaction only angered Jenna more so she walked away.

As they left the room, Louis came closer to them screaming now,

"Amy was buried? Where? You got the wrong guy! I didn't bury her! YOU HEAR ME! YOU GOT THE WRONG-"

The cops restrained him and just as they were walking away, Jenna and Mark both received a text.

The coroner's office. The autopsy was taking more time than expected but they had completed Stella's report and sent it. Amy's report was yet to come in. The cause of death for Stella was identified. Blunt force trauma to the head. The estimated time since death also matches Louis' side of the story. The pregnancy was also confirmed. Their final steps await.

Jenna and Mark decide to go ahead with the arrest despite the delayed autopsy report of Amy. They decided to make the arrests and let the district attorney's office take care of the rest.

The night finally rested with peace for the both of them. A final closure to a dreadful many weeks. Both Christopher and Louis arrested as accomplices in the double homicide of Amy and Stella. Case closed.

As Jenna headed home that night, she felt as if something was lifted off her shoulders. She felt at ease. She could finally have a good night's sleep after weeks. Or so she thought. Her not-so-peaceful sleep was cut short. The daunting images of Amy and Stella kept coming back at her.

She woke up from her sleep, gasping for breath and found herself all heated and covered in sweat. She took a moment to catch her breath. Her phone on the bed stand nearby was vibrating so she took it to see who was calling her in the middle of the night so late. It was the coroner's office. She took the call all surprised coz she didn't expect it. The caller on the other side sounded urgent,

"Hey Jen, did I wake you? Is this a bad time?"

"No... Ummm... what's up? Why'd you call?"

"Yea well... I know the case is closed now and all... I was asked to keep this a secret as well... but I felt like you should know... It is about Amy."

"Yea, what's wrong? Was there something else we missed?"

"I mean, yea. Ummm... we did find another hair strand of a female from the body but that's not the weird part."

"A female? You sure? What else?"

"Ok, don't make a big deal out of this alright coz we were specifically asked to keep this to ourselves. Directly from the district attorney's office. But am letting you know as a friend. Just don't act harshly and maybe like... take it at ease... and find out more..."

Getting annoyed with the unnecessarily lengthened call, Jenna asked what the actual reason behind the call was. The officer replied,

"Amy's estimated time of death was what we noted first which seemed out of place. She died only a couple of hours before being found. The accused was already in custody by that time... so we got digging to find out how that was possible. Things that could've led to her death were plenty, clear signs of sexual assault, blunt force trauma, excessive blood loss, severe case of dehydration... but that's not it. The actual cause of death was... asphyxiation, with traces of mud and dust particles in her."

Confused and all awake, Jenna asked,

"So what does that have to do with anything?"

The officer finally got to the point with a tough sigh,

"Amy... she... she was buried alive."

CHAPTER V

Weeks later, the entire town seemed to have moved on. The court's final verdict restored peace and harmony for everyone and claimed justice for both Amy and Stella.

Slowly, by the support of the society, family and friends, Stella's parents and Linda were trying to move on with their life as well. There were murals painted in memory of Amy and Stella, where Linda was a frequent visitor.

Bit by bit, everything seemed to be falling back in place. Even at the station, this particular case had changed everybody's lives. The chief got his time shining in the spotlight before his retirement. The entire station were praised for their work and received a lot of considerable attention. Mark and Jen were promoted too.

Everybody were happy and satisfied with everything. Or so it seemed. Except for one. Jenna.

Jenna couldn't move on. Not from everything that happened. Not with everything she saw. She thought getting the closure she needed and getting those criminals punished would bring her peace and let her move on. But she never did.

Still haunted by their faces, the case somehow remained in Jenna's head as a ticking time bomb. Not going off in any set time but triggering her with that fear increasing every minute of every day.

Something didn't seem right to her. Amy's autopsy result was what made it all more frustrating to Jenna. An unidentified female's DNA and being buried alive. She couldn't leave out the possibility of Louis not being the actual murderer in the case and that thought kept torturing her. The thought of the actual murderer still being out there.

Every day she would show up at the station and as she sat in her office, she'd get upset over the smallest things leading to panic attacks making her all nervous and short of breath.

It was as if she was experiencing being locked in a small space and having no way out. The fear made her unable to move or do anything at all. After a few recurring episodes of the scare at her office, she made sure to distract herself every day with work.

More cases and more people to distract her mind and keep it busy. But at the end of the day, she would get all exhausted. It gets way into her head to the point where she finds herself passed out at different places without any recollection of how she got there in the first place.

Things started to get way out of hand as time passed. Jenna was aware of it too. She was caught between herself and her guilt. The guilt she felt for not finding out the truth. For not finding out about Amy's final moments' reality.

Jenna finally decided to reach out to someone. She thought this person would be of most help… or of least harm. At least it help her get rid of some of the guilt she was feeling.

She walked into a house, rang the doorbell and someone answered the door.

"Hello Jenna. Long time. Why don't you come in and have a seat."

Feeling a bit relieved already, she replied,

"Hi, Linda."

Walking into her house with a sunken heart, Jenna was really there for help. As she walked through the living room, towards the dining hall, she couldn't help but notice all of Amy's pictures put up on the walls.

They were not there the first time she visited for the routine interviews of the case. It was as if Linda remodeled the entire house to a one-of-a-kind Amy shrine!

"You've been keeping busy by decorating, I see"

Looking at Jenna admiring Amy's photos, Linda smiled softly and replied,

"Yea. Funny thing. She was always mad about how I never had any of her photos up anywhere. Ah, the fits she used to throw around..."

Jenna was smiling looking at Linda now,

"She'd be happy seeing this now... from somewhere..."

Linda just nodded and didn't know what to say.

Jenna kept looking around and for the first time, saw a family photo with an unfamiliar person holding a toddler Amy. Assuming it to be Amy's father, she asked,

"If you don't mind me asking, what happened to Amy's father?"

Linda walked towards her, took the photo frame in her hands and again, with a soft smile reminiscing all the good old memories, said

"A car accident... Oh, he was a sweetheart. A pure soul indeed. Maybe that's why he was called in too soon. How the purest of souls leave this world too soon... that goes for him. And my sweet little Amy too. I just didn't want her to suffer that much. She didn't... didn't deserve... such a painful end."

Stuttering for words, Linda was now silently sobbing.

Jenna immediately tried to change subjects and asked if the kettle was on hearing it from the kitchen. Linda got the tea ready and the two was having a peaceful time. Linda started the conversation again,

"You know how happy we would be right now if Amy's dad was still around..."

Jenna just smiled along while Linda kept speaking,

"Or... how things would be if I never welcomed that bastard into our lives... oh... my poor Amy... All she had to go through..."

Jenna suddenly had a lot of questions to ask but didn't know if it was right to ask them right away. Never the less, she asked

"But why did you? I mean... before getting together with him... you must have known about his true nature..."

Linda shocked to hear Jenna's question, asked by leaning forward to her,

"Did you honestly think I called him in? Dated him? Married him for love? Really?"

Surprised by her sudden outburst, Jenna asked why she married him if not for any personal reason. After a moment of silence, she took in a deep breath and said,

"Amy. It was all to protect Amy."

Astonished by what she just heard, Jenna asked,

"Excuse me, WHAT?"

Linda, heavily sighed and began telling her story.

"It was all in vain. Everything I did. Everything I sacrificed. Everything I put up with till now. Louis. That bastard. He used to follow me around when Amy was only a kid. He used to be there everywhere. I rejected him every time he asked me out so that seemed to have angered him quite a bit! The stalking only got worse... some times, he used to be there at Amy's nursery even when I wasn't there! That's when I confronted him and told him if he wasn't gona stop, I would get the cops involved. Instead of being scared or intimidated, he was threatening me. When his threats got more and more

concerning, I asked him what I could do to make him leave us alone. He made a promise to me that day. He told me he was never going to leave us alone... but... but if I married him... if he had me to himself... then he'd leave Amy alone. He said he wouldn't harm her. He said as long as I was there by his side, he wouldn't dare do anything to my daughter... but if I were to reject him again...or get the cops involved... then I wouldn't see her at all..."

Completely shook to her core, Jenna was out of words to say anything. Linda continued after taking a moment to wipe her tears.

"I made a decision that day. I decided to be right beside him for the rest of his life to always have an eye on him. Little did I know, my choices came with all of the consequences I couldn't handle. All these years... all this time... and how oblivious I have been... I knew from the start there were gona be all kinds of struggles getting in to this relationship with him... but I made sure to remind him of his own words every now and then. Even if he didn't care for a thing in the world, he took the weight of his own words pretty seriously. I did it all, sacrificed myself for years... only to make sure Amy was safe from him at all costs. Even though I expected him to cross his own words once, I never thought it would all come to this."

Linda broke down in tears with unbearable pain.

Jenna finally spoke,

"It wasn't all for nothing. Amy's not here to see it but you did everything you could. And him... he is serving for his crimes now. You have nothing to be guilty for."

Linda scuffed at Jenna's last comment and said,

"You wouldn't know the half of it. I didn't raise my daughter as I wanted. I didn't provide enough for her. Didn't give her enough attention. Or even let her know how much I loved her. How much I still do. All because I was busy trying to keep her from all the evil in this very house. And after all that... she

ended up in his hands after all... There is no way to bring my girl back. There is no one I can send to bring her back. There is no way to retrieve her. This sorrow, it keeps cutting deep into my heart. At times, this grief strikes me so hard I just want to go to her. To wherever she is right now..."

Sobbing so painfully hard, Linda stopped talking.

Jenna was in an attempt to make sure Linda doesn't have any more crazy ideas in her head,

"Whenever you think of something like that... to risk your life to do something dumb... just think of her. Think of Amy. Imagine what she would be doing right now. How she would feel seeing you like this. How she-"

Interrupting her midsentence, Linda shouted

"THINK... THINK ABOUT HER?"

Jenna was taken back with the sudden outburst and got all silent. Linda lowered her voice and resumed speaking

"THAT'S ALL I EVER DO!!! EVERY SECOND OF EVERY DAY! Everything I couldn't do for her... everything I put her through... and everything I did do to her. It's everything that I have ever done that makes it impossible for me to ever face her again."

Jenna was all confused now. She just sat there, staring at a crying guilt filled Linda.

What was supposed to be a time to help Jenna... to somehow relieve herself from all the guilt she was feeling herself, had now turned tables. However she did have her mind distracted for a while trying to console Linda.

Comparing one's sorrow or grief to someone else's is something unreliable. Jenna knew that. Different people have different sides of their stories to tell... different ways to feel the pain and cope with it too. She was experiencing it firsthand.

She thought her darkness was nothing compared to what

Linda was going through.

Feeling more lost than ever, she didn't know how to handle her own emotions.

Caught up trying to help someone else navigate through their tough times, she forgot to focus on herself. Unable to find a way out from the torture she was putting herself through, Jenna finally opened up to Linda.

She caught Linda's hand which rested on the sofa beside her and slowly started to let out her emotions,

"To be honest Linda... I am having a hard time. I can't... I don't... don't know how to explain it. I just feel this heavy weight pulling me down. Every. Single. Day. I can't get myself out of this. I feel like I should've done more. For Amy. For you. This... this feeling... this guilt... it's eating me alive."

Linda, ever so surprised to hear the open confession, stood up, took Jenna into her arms and hugged her. She didn't say a word. She let her actions speak.

Jenna didn't know how to react. She felt less burdened. She hugged Linda back and before she knew it, tears were rolling down her face.

They stood there, in utter silence, both of them in tears, just letting their broken dismantled hearts find some solemn peace from each other's embrace.

As time went by, Jenna decided to head home after having dinner with her. Over dinner, not much was said. Somehow, they felt each other's presence comforting enough.

As their time together was coming to an end, Jenna wanted Linda to know how thankful she was, for being there for her despite being in pain herself. She said

"Thank you for today Linda. I needed this. I needed someone there for me. Thanks."

Linda smiled and hugged her again.

Jenna, before leaving, wanted to confess something else,

"Hey... Ummm... I know its way past the time for this but... but... am sorry. I really am. If we were a little faster, if we had found her a bit quicker... maybe... maybe things would've been different today..."

Jenna didn't know what reaction she was expecting but weirdly Linda was unfazed. As she opened the door, Linda nodded and said,

"Had you guys found her earlier... there would be no difference. Could've been worse really. Even if you guys did, there would've been nothing for Amy to go on with her life in that state. Let's not talk about all that's done. Now, you take care Jenna."

They bid each other goodbyes and left in their own ways.

Jen was out the door and walking towards her car when she suddenly stopped. Her body froze. It was like she was having another meltdown episode coming in. But this time, it was different. Something didn't seem right. Something kept bothering her. Suddenly a lot of voices started echoing in her head... different voices, all at once...

"I didn't bury Amy. You got the wrong guy. Hair strand of an unidentified female. Amy... she... she was buried alive. She didn't deserve it. Even if you guys did, there would've been nothing for Amy to go on with her life in that state."

Jenna's head was hurting as if the time bomb was finally set to blow. With the unbearable pain, she was down on her knees in the front yard of Amy's house. She felt like she was about to pass out. Now that her panic attack was also coming in, she was gasping for breath.

A flashback of the day when Louis was apprehended was playing in Jenna's head. Mark's voice was echoing now,

"Linda's supposed to be here. I don't see her anywhere though."

That's it.

Jenna opened her eyes. She slowly stood up. Even with an unbearable headache, she started connecting the dots. Step by step… hesitatingly… she started walking back to the door she just came out of, nervously trembling to face Linda now, Jenna rang the doorbell. Answering the door, Linda asked,

"Did you forget something Jenna?"

Jenna didn't say anything and just stared at her.

Confused by her behavior, Linda asked if she was ok and if something was wrong.

Holding back a thousand conflicting emotions, Jenna finally asked,

"Where were you the day we caught Louis?"

Linda was not as strong as she pretended to be on the outside. She tried to hide it but she knew the purpose of Jenna's question. She didn't want to play dumb. She didn't want anyone to draw any conclusions either.

What was seemingly a welcoming pleasant face, in an instant… changed to a sad pitiful pale one. She took Jenna in, closed the door and took a seat.

"I knew someone would eventually find out..."

Linda's words astonished Jen.

"W... Wh... What? Are you... are you confessing to something?"

Linda looked at Jenna with dreadful eyes filled with tears and asked,

"If I did… Would Louis just walk? Won't he be freed? Like he didn't do anything to my girl…"

"Linda… please… tell me you didn't… please… just… what did you do?"

She looked at Jenna, hesitated for a while, bit her lips in despair and finally started talking,

"Every day I used to follow you guys at the station. Every time you and Mark left the station... getting a call

or something... I'd be right behind you... I wanted to make sure for myself if it was just a dead end or some way to find Amy... but I always made sure not to get caught or get noticed by you. I couldn't risk it before finding her. That day...when everyone headed to the woods to catch Louis... I was there too. I saw you guys heading to the woods. I saw how you guys took him back to the station and everything. I even saw the search parties with all those people getting ready to go in... But everything was taking a lot of time! Everything was so annoyingly slow and reckless. So I went in myself. To the woods. Through the trail you all came out of. It was just an instinct. I just... I knew exactly where to go. I followed my instincts... and... and... I found that bunker..."

Linda got all silent and was now staring at the photo frame on the table, the family photo of her, with just tears flowing down her cheeks.

Trying to take in everything she was hearing, Jenna didn't speak a word either.

Holding back more tears, Linda continued,

"I knew what I was going to walk into... but I... I just... I didn't expect to see her like that! I opened the door and I saw her. Lying there. On the floor. I can still see her face, right here, in front of me..."

Even with all the frustration Jenna was feeling, she could see the pain in Linda's eyes as she spoke. She softly held Linda's hand on the table as she was struggling to say anything at all.

"I wanted to scream. Call out for help. Get her somewhere safe. I wanted to. Really did. But... but... my phone... As I sat there unable to do anything at all, my phone got busy with a lot of calls and texts. I took it to call you guys. To tell you I found her. To call someone. Anyone. But... I saw what everyone was saying. The messages and everything. The news headlines people were sending me. Everything. Every message, every

news article, each text I was getting was horrible. It was all just a mayhem."

Jenna broke her long awaited silence,

"News? What are you talking about?"

Getting frustrated by the second, Jenna didn't understand what was going on.

Linda took out her phone and showed all the news articles she had received on that day…

Jenna was aware of the fact that the media manipulation was involved but she didn't actually check out any of the published articles herself. But after she went through a few of them showed by Linda, she was both shocked and disgusted by what she was reading.

Linda slowly got up, walked towards one of Amy's photos on the wall, stared at the happy smiling girl in the photo, and said

"Everything they were saying. Every word they were saying about my girl... when she was... on the floor... helplessly lying there unconscious..."

Linda took a moment to wipe her tears and continued,

"There was one particular article that said something about extra marital affair between a teenager and her stepfather. I just did not understand what people were thinking. I didn't understand what they were doing. I didn't understand why they were focused on ending my daughter's life when she was already hanging onto it barely. I realized it then. If they were saying all that before they even saw what he did to her. If they were capable of saying all those things even before knowing what she had gone through... imagine... imagine what they would say after... imagine what they were capable of doing after. I... I couldn't... I couldn't knowingly bring my girl back to life only for her to live the rest of it in terror. As a scapegoat. Being eaten alive."

With fearful teary eyes, Linda turned back at Jen and with

a determined look she said,

"For the rest of her life, she wouldn't be able to sleep one night without all of this... all this torture... everything she'd been through... haunting her. Had I saved her that day... it would have only been a selfish cruel deed on my end. I couldn't let my girl go through hell. Not after what she'd been through. Not again."

Jenna stood up as she couldn't bring up the courage to say anything and approached Linda. Silently looking into her eyes Linda put on a faded smile and whispered,

"In the end, I did what I had to do."

THE DAY AMY WAS FOUND

In a world full of sadness, redemptions and second chances at life, Linda contemplated every possible outcome that could come out after saving Amy. Even if she lives after being taken out of that horror house, Linda wondered if her daughter will ever get a chance to live a normal life again. She thought to herself if it was fair for her to decide and let Amy live on for years with all of these terrifying memories and trauma to haunt her.

A broken mother in an attempt to save her daughter, decides to save her life by ending it.

Linda hugged Amy for a long time, wept and kept cursing at herself for everything she couldn't do- everything she had done- everything she was about to do.

Lastly, with little to no strength or power in herself, she gets up with Amy still in her arms and places her gently on the floor. She goes out of the bunker, takes the shovel that was already there in the corner and started digging.

Crying, screaming and her heart breaking into a million pieces with every single step she took, she doesn't stop.

Linda goes back into the bunker filthy, covered in mud

and dirt all over her, with tears in her eyes that won't stop. Linda carries Amy out. Coming out of the dark bunker, the light outside gave a clearer image of Amy's tormented face from which her mother broke down again.

Screaming, holding her daughter in her arms, Linda couldn't decide on anything. She paused for a minute and thought of ending things all together. By taking her life along with Amy's. Ending everything for the both of them.

That thought only lasted a minute when she realized she couldn't do that yet. Not until Louis gets what he deserves. Not until she could see him suffer. Not until she made sure he was held accountable for everything he put Amy through.

Linda decided that only then, only after settling things once and for all, will she return to her beloved daughter.

THE PRESENT DAY

Jenna lived her entire life abiding by the law. She knew nothing but to live by the system. However, for the first time in her life, she was doubting the very bane of her existence. She didn't know if she could go on with her life as is.

It's been two days since she learnt of the truth behind Amy's death.

Being a detective, she is supposed to know what to do in situations like these… except… she was completely lost at this point. Unable to make a decision to handle it, Jenna makes a decision for herself instead.

Filled with all kinds of emotions and unanswered questions, Jenna enters the station with a folded up envelope in her hand. As she makes her way through the station, she unexpectedly bumps into Mark.

They were no longer partners so they didn't meet each other as often as they used to. Mark tried to reach out to her a couple of times even after their split.

To him, Jenna was his only hope, a support system and his

only form of sanity. He wanted to have an open conversation with her after their hectic case, but unable to express what he was going through himself, things between them eventually just got awkward.

"Hey Jen... Ummm... Where are you headed?"

Mark tried to start a conversation with Jenna trying to get things between them back to normal.

Jenna, on the other hand, was already in a hurry to get things done. She didn't stay long to catch up with him and said,

"It was good working with you Mark. Thank you for being there for me. Good times and the bad ones. I'll be rooting for you... from afar! Good luck!"

Something about the way she spoke sounded like a final goodbye to him. Confusingly flustered, he asked her what was going on but there was no reply.

A clueless Mark was left in the dark. She thought it'd be better for him if he didn't know anything about what she recently discovered about their case.

Jenna smiled, hugged him one last time and whispered in his ears,

"Good bye Mark. I'll try to keep in touch."

Baffled and upset with Jenna's sudden revelation, Mark just stood there and watched her walk away.

Jenna entered the Chief's office, placed her resignation letter on his desk and without any explanations or any more last minute goodbyes, left the station. Forever.

CHAPTER VI

THROUGH AMY'S EYES

People should just stop existing. Really. Mass extinction. Just complete human extinction will do a lot of people a lot of good! I honestly don't know why we are living in a society where monsters like him get to feed on others like me.

Amy was physically and mentally exhausted out of reach. Days and weeks long of torture has taken an irreversible toll on her!

I shouldn't have come here. I shouldn't have asked him about Stella. I shouldn't have tried to find her on my own. I shouldn't have left home that day. I don't even know how long it has been since then.

Oh mom, where are you? Why is no one coming to help me? Am I forgotten too? Just like Stella? Doesn't anyone care about us to come and get me out of here?

The amount of times I've wished to be dead here but wow, I don't want to die here. Oh please. Someone. Anyone. Get me out of here.

Although I am not entirely sure if I am alive at this point. I cannot move a single muscle in my body nor can I open my eyes. No matter how hard I try… nothing works.

At first, I could feel the pain. I could feel everything he did to me. I was able to resist him. I could scream out for help. I could scream out in pain too. Now I can't. It's like every last bit of energy or my life itself has drained out of my body.

I don't even know what happens to me now. What he does to me. Everything is numb. I can only hear stuff. That's all there is. Sounds.

I can hear him come and go. But now that I don't feel anything, his presence doesn't scare me anymore. I just hope I get out of here someday.

I've lost track of time so I don't know how long I've been here… a week maybe? More than that perhaps?

I feel like my mom might come to rescue me any day now… so yea, am holding on to that. I can't give up. Not until I see her again. Oh, how sorry I feel for her. I used to say to her that I hate her for everything. Ignore her for no reason. I thought she was the reason I was hurting. I used to think I was the one suffering every day.

What hell had she had to go through, to have lived with this guy all this time?

Mom, if only I could call out for you. To tell you how sorry I am. To tell you how thankful I am to have you. I should've told you how much I love you. I don't remember the last time I did. Oh please. Don't let me die here. I need to tell her at least once!

Wait, I hear something… I guess he is back. I don't reckon there's much for me to do about that though. Wait… what… who… why's the sound different? Is that a woman? Is it someone else who stumbled upon here by mistake?

Oh… whoever you are… help… help me!! Please!! How can I say it out loud…? I… I am trying… Please… Please don't leave. I am in here. Please. Help.

Amy could hear someone screaming and mumbling a lot of words but couldn't quite make of what was being said.

Ok wait. I have heard this voice before… why does it sound familiar?

Am I hallucinating things now? Is this delusional voices I am hearing? Wait… if it's not, what are you saying? Who is this? Why do you sound familiar to me? Did you call the cops by the way?

Quick, I guess we need to get out of here before we are both dead meat. Just stop screaming and do something or call someone.

How do I let this person know what's really happening?

Wait a minute… this voice… m… mom? Is that you? Are you here? Mo... Mom? Why am I hearing your voice here? Is this real?

Can someone wake me from all of this if this is all just a big nightmare? Mom, is that really you? Can I really believe it's you?

Wait… why does this sound different than before? Am I in a different place now? Am I out of there? Am I saved? Why is there no one else around though? Why am I not hearing any siren or people? Why is it oddly silent?

Am I actually just delusional at this point? Did I just make it up for myself like as if I heard my mother's sound? Am I really that far gone? Will I ever be saved to return back to my life again?

W… wait… why is it getting more silent? Why can't I hear anything? Why does it feel different? Why am I not able to breath?

Was it actually him again? Am I going to die? Is he finally putting an end to all this? To me? Am I really dying here? Today? Now? But… but… I'm not ready… I… I want to meet my mom… tell her I love her. W…Why… did it have to be today? Why me? It's getting harder for me to breathe… I can feel that.

I don't know what he is doing to me but at least I'm not

hearing his voice anymore. Be it delusional or not, I got to hear my mom's voice. I got to hear her voice as my last sound. I am satisfied with that.

I guess it is better for her to not see me like this. I don't think she will be able to handle it. I guess this works out for the best of us. Hopefully, he will make sure that I am not found. I don't want her to be in pain after I am gone.

Mom, take care. Wherever you are, I want you to know I love you. I always did and I always will.

Amy's final thoughts were only of her mother. Hoping that her mother would find peace without her. Hoping her mother would move on with her life pretending like nothing ever happened, because she thought she would never be found. She thought that her mother would never know of what had actually happened to her.

If only she were to realize the voice she heard was in fact her mother's and not a delusion. The fact that her final moments were right beside her own mother. Maybe it all worked out for the best with Amy thinking her mother's voice was a delusion and Linda thinking her daughter was unconscious the entire time. For that was better than knowing for sure that Amy was being buried alive by her own mother.

Some feelings are so painfully personal that when they are expressed, they don't last forever.

Why not have some faith in fate?